SPINOZA'S RADICAL THEOLOGY

SPINOZA'S RADICAL THEOLOGY

The Metaphysics of the Infinite

Charlie Huenemann

Routledge

Taylor & Francis Group

LONDON AND NEW YORK

First published 2014 by Acumen

Published 2014 by Routledge
2 Park Square, Milton Park, Abingdon, Oxon OX14 4RN
711 Third Avenue, New York, NY 10017, USA

Routledge is an imprint of the Taylor & Francis Group, an informa business

ISBN: 978-1-84465-578-6 (hardcover)
ISBN: 978-1-84465-579-3 (paperback)

British Library Cataloguing-in-Publication Data
A catalogue record for this book is available from the British Library.

Typeset in Warnock Pro.

Dedicated to my theological uncles:
Ruben, Edward, Lorenz, Robert, and William

Contents

Acknowledgements

I owe thanks to many. Parts of this work have been presented to the 2010 Spinoza Conference in Kingston, Ontario, and to a Spinoza workshop hosted by the University of Ghent. I thank those organizers, and the participants at those conferences for criticisms and suggestions. A more general thanks is due to Eric Schliesser, who has kindly shown encouragement for all of my work over the past seven years. Still more longstanding thanks, for many instructive insights and dialogues about Spinoza's philosophy, are due to Tom Cook, Edwin Curley, Michael Della Rocca, Michael Griffin, Daniel Garber, Don Garrett, Steven Nadler, Michael Rosenthal and Don Rutherford. More recently, two reviewers of the manuscript provided constructive criticism and advice, for which I thank them, whoever they are. Tristan Palmer, at Acumen, has shown truly remarkable patience and faith ("assurance of things hoped for, the conviction of things not seen"). Utah State University has supported my work without complaint for nearly two decades, which is beneficence I do not take for granted. And to my family – well, of course, it goes without saying.

Abbreviations

Curley   Various works by Spinoza, as found in *The Collected Works of Spinoza*, volume I, E. Curley (ed. and trans.) (Princeton, NJ: Princeton University Press, 1985). These include *Korte Verhandling van God, de Mensch en des Zelfs Welstand* (*Short Treatise on God, Man, and His Well-Being*) (c. 1660); *Tractatus de Intellectus Emendatione* (*Treatise on the Emendation of the Intellect*) (c. 1662, unfinished); *Renati Des Cartes Principiorum Philosophiae* (*Principles of Cartesian Philosophy*), along with its appendix "Cogitata Metaphysica" ("Metaphysical Thoughts") (1663).

Ethics   Spinoza, *Ethica Ordina Geometrico Demonstrata* (1677), as found in *The Collected Works of Spinoza*, volume I, E. Curley (ed. and trans.) (Princeton, NJ: Princeton University Press, 1985). Passages are cited by part, proposition, scholium and so on, so that "*Ethics* IP20c2" refers to part I, proposition 20, second corollary.

Leibniz/Loemker   Leibniz, *Philosophical Papers and Letters*, L. Loemker (trans.), 2nd edn/second printing (Dordrecht: Kluwer, [1666–1716] 1989).

Letters   Spinoza's letters (1661–76), as found in *The Letters*, S. Shirley (trans.) (Indianapolis, IN: Hackett, 1995). Passages are cited by number of the letter, and the name of the correspondent.

Political Spinoza, *Tractatus Politicus* (1676, unfinished), as found in *Political Treatise*, S. Shirley (trans.) (Indianapolis, IN: Hackett, 2000). Passages are cited by chapter and section.

Theological-Political Spinoza, *Tractatus Theologico-Politicus* (1670), as found in *Theological-Political Treatise*, M. Silverthorne & J. Israel (trans.) (Cambridge: Cambridge University Press, 2007). Passages are cited by chapter and section.

References to the Bible are to the Revised Standard Version.

Preface

Does that man, pray, renounce all religion, who declares that God must be acknowledged as the highest good, and that he must be loved as such in a free spirit? And that in this alone does our supreme happiness and our highest freedom consist? And further, that the reward of virtue is virtue itself, while the punishment of folly and weakness is folly itself? And lastly, that everyone is in duty bound to love his neighbor and obey the commands of the sovereign power? I not only said this explicitly, but also proved it with the strongest arguments.

(*Letters* 43, to Velthuysen)

It is tempting to read Spinoza as a philosopher who tried to distance himself from religion. After all, although he argues for the existence of an immutable and eternal substance he calls "God", this substance has no personal features and no concern for the welfare of humanity. And although he argues for the eternality of the mind, this eternality is nothing like an afterlife in which the just are rewarded and the unjust punished. He argues against even the possibility of miracles, and he regards scripture as "erroneous, mutilated, corrupt and inconsistent" (*Theological-Political* 12.1). If he had founded a church it is hard to see what the parishioners would do in it, apart from learning geometry, metaphysics and the natural and social sciences.

But, of course, it is also true that Spinoza did not distance himself from religion as much as he might have. He could have come right out and said:

> In truth, God does not exist. There is a deep unity in nature, which has some features that match ones traditionally ascribed to God, but this deep unity is so impersonal that we would be better off not calling it "God" at all, so as to avoid unnecessary confusion.

Spinoza, that is, could have been an outright and plain-spoken atheist who found a thrilling but non-divine unity in the natural world. Indeed, that daring position would not have been much more problematic than the one he did espouse. But instead – as I hope to show – he consistently sought to salvage as much as he possibly could from ancient religion, and to *correct* our notion of God rather than abandon it.

Now some scholars might maintain that this was some kind of failure on Spinoza's part: he did not think through to the genuine consequences of his philosophy, or he was, for whatever reason, unable to bring himself to face those consequences. No less a Spinoza scholar than the great H. A. Wolfson thought this:

> That Spinoza himself was not fully conscious of his own radical departure, that he speaks of the opposition to his views as due to "the prejudices of the theologians" and of the "atheism" with which the common people accused him as an untrue accusation, that he continues to consider himself a successor of the religious thinkers of the past who tried to discover the truth that lay hidden in the pages of Scripture, and that he occasionally speaks of his God in the pious phrases of tradition – all this is due to the inherent tendency of men to rationalize and accommodate old beliefs to their own thought. His reputed God-intoxication was really nothing but a hang-over of an earlier religious jag. ([1934] 1962: II, 348)[1]

xiv

But Wolfson's appraisal can be turned on its head: *given* that Spinoza did consistently reject the accusation of atheism, and *given* that he saw himself as a successor to the religious thinkers of the past, and *given* that he occasionally – no, very frequently, and with poetic elegance – speaks of God in pious phrases of tradition: given all this, is it not more reasonable to see Spinoza as presenting not an alternative to religion, but a further rationalistic reform of religion? Rather than seeing him as continuing to suffer from a hangover he was unable to shake, shouldn't we see him as someone trying to elucidate the truth he saw at the core of the tradition in which he was raised?

Within the last generation or so, several scholars have begun to read Spinoza in this way, namely as a religious reformer rather than as one presenting a complete rejection of religion.[2] This book shares this approach, and offers an interpretation of Spinoza's whole philosophy – including his reading of scripture (Chapter 1), his metaphysics (Chapter 2), his view of nature and science (Chapter 3), his psychology (Chapter 4) and his politics (Chapter 5) – as a radical theology. Spinoza had a conception of God and an account of how God is responsible for the existence of all things; he had a view of human morality, and politics, that was grounded in his theology; and he advanced this theology not merely as an atheistic metaphysics that could be slyly promoted to the masses through duplicitous usages of religious terms, but as a *genuine* theology. He thought his philosophy was bringing into clarity ancient insights that were distorted through prejudices, ignorance and superstition. Spinoza believed the ancient prophets somehow glimpsed, "as if through a cloud", as he writes (*Ethics* IIP7S), many important truths: that there is a divine agency at work in the world, that love of God is our highest good, that we are in God and God in us, that we should love one another, and so on. It is just that the ancient prophets were in no position to see *why* any of this should be true. And that, in the end, is the virtue of scripture: it is able to impart truths without a complete understanding of them. The virtue of philosophy lies in its ability to provide a complete understanding, which Spinoza took himself to have done.

Thus, according to this book's perspective, Spinoza should not be portrayed as "an enemy from without", or the atheistic Jew of

Amsterdam who attacks the rationality of religion overall, but instead as a philosopher attempting to reform religion from within, bringing his readers or students to see in it deeper truths that are consonant with modern philosophical naturalism. Spinoza's goal, in other words, is to find something divine in the world, and even in scripture, that good modernists can still believe in.

This ambition should be of philosophical interest today. For our religious debates are typically framed as a choice between naturalism and religion. Spinoza saw the divine in nature; indeed, it is not too much to say that he did not think nature could be understood completely without grasping its divinity. This is not to say there are ever any miracles, or anything cloaked in the inscrutable nature of God. It is to say that the study of nature, understood to its clear depths, will reveal something divine. That is, to say the least, an interesting possibility. In the conclusion I shall pit Spinoza's divine naturalism against the robust atheistic naturalism of Nietzsche, which is the kind of naturalism subscribed to by the naturalists of today, whether they are willing to see it or not!

I should say something here at the start about why I am concerned to present this reading of Spinoza. Spinoza's philosophy is one of the greatest ever conceived, and I have devoted large portions of my adult life to understanding it (among other things); and I think reading his philosophy as an overall attempt at constructing a theology is the best way of reading him. I hope this book advances that understanding. Alongside this, I have the belief that contemporary philosophical naturalists need to think carefully about all they are abandoning, and should proceed with greater caution. I hope this book contributes in a small way to this cautionary note by providing an accurate portrait of another variety of naturalism that does not abandon quite so much. The naturalists among us face a critical decision about how to regard nature. Is it as an arbitrary lodging or a kind of sanctuary? That is a question as alive for us as it was for Spinoza. It is perhaps, in the end, the deepest question anyone can ask.

Introduction

Spinoza's theological project

Then I prove that the revealed word of God is not a certain
number of books but a pure conception of the divine mind
which was revealed by the prophets, namely, to obey God
with all one's mind by practising justice and charity.

(Theological-Political preface 10)

A PARABLE

Imagine one day encountering a civilization foreign to ours, with
advanced technology and a seemingly accurate grasp of nature. Its
citizens engage in public discourse, debating over the way their
society should run and what policies should be enacted. They have
a good understanding of their own bodies and their own psycholo-
gies, advanced enough for them to know their own strengths and
many of their own blind spots and weaknesses. They are careful
not to waste or spoil their natural resources, and live in a kind of
harmony with their environment. They are, in almost every respect,
what we might call an "enlightened" citizenry, in the sense that they
try to behave reasonably and they try to sort out what they should
believe in intelligent and impartial ways, all against a common
backdrop of mutual concern for one another and goodwill.

But one feature of this civilization is especially striking. In the centre of their major city is a small cave, which is widely regarded by the citizens as sacred. The city's major buildings form a ring around it, and its principal streets lead to it from the four compass points. In the cave are found ancient writings scratched into the wall. No one knows exactly when they were made, or who made them, or for what reason and in what set of circumstances. The language of the scratchings has been deciphered for the most part, although there remain many ambiguities and uncertainties. The scratchings record many ancient stories, some of them wildly fantastic, some of them perhaps rooted in some historical fact and many of them simply bizarre and baffling. There are also portions of the cave text that prescribe rules to human beings, ranging from "Be kind to your offspring" to "Never feed a goat on a moonless night".

As it turns out, many Cavenians (for we may as well give them a name) try to orient their lives around the prescriptions found in the cave, and they devote a portion of their time to studying the cave-scratchings and venerating the characters described in the stories. Some of them profess to believe every story recounted in the cave, even when the stories seem to contradict one another or the proper understanding of nature. There are deep and developed controversies over how to interpret the scratchings, and it is here that the normally civil discourse of this advanced civilization has sometimes broken down. For there is a history of Cavenians attacking one another and even murdering one another over matters of interpretation. Even today polite conversation tends to avoid certain topics lest the old tempers flare once again. Only recently has it been possible to confess publicly that one does not believe the cave is at all sacred without fearing some sort of reprisal.

The Cavenians' devotion to the cave is hard for us to understand. They ought to know, given their understanding of history and human psychology, that people who lived long ago did not have an accurate understanding of the world around them, and often invented mythological stories to help them feel as if they did understand. (Indeed, this is precisely how the Cavenians themselves describe the ancient religions of *other* cultures.) They ought to know that a moral teaching does not become more authoritative in virtue of being scratched into stone. And, when it comes to the violence associated with interpretations, they ought to know that writings – and especially ancient ones, in languages not fully understood – can bear multiple interpretations, and those who disagree are not necessarily lesser human beings on that account. Just why the Cavenians revere the cave is a mystery to us since it seems to be so much at odds with the otherwise quite reasonable and intelligent ways they conduct themselves in their advanced civilization.

When we ask them about their devotion, they tell us that they believe the writings are not simply ancient scratchings. The writings, they believe, are messages that come from the Source of All Good Things. This Source put order into the world, which makes their advanced civilization possible. The Source imparted its message to the Cavenians because it has concern for them and wants them to live full and rich lives. Moreover, the Source has promised that there is some sort of immortal existence for anyone who properly heeds the message. When we ask the Cavenians how they know all this, they begin to recite passages from the cave-scratchings. The scratchings, it turns out, say a great deal about the Source although little of it is clear and not all of it is consistent. We point out that what is said in the scratchings cannot possibly serve as *reason* for believing in the truth of the scratchings – that a text cannot lift itself up by its own bootstraps, as it were, and prove itself to be true – but they dismiss this objection. Many of them feel in their hearts that what is in the cave is true, and they also feel that their lives are better when lived according to the cave's teachings than when they try to ignore those teachings.

As we examine the cave's teachings in greater detail, we find that we must admit that there is a good deal of sensible advice in them. There is the occasional strange teaching (such as the one about not feeding goats), but many of the teachings offer good rules to live by: be honest in all your dealings; help out those in need; revere every natural thing as a gift from the Source; do not let the sun set without a kind deed done to your neighbour; listen to your neighbour with a cool brow; and so on. And, it seems, the Cavenians on the whole have established a decent community (apart from the history of violent and murderous disagreements over interpretation, of course; but contemporary Cavenians now also disapprove of those violent acts).

Perhaps, we will admit, there is a sense in which the cave-scratchings have provided the Cavenians with something that is true: not "true" in any straightforward sense, since to us it is obvious that the scratchings must have been written by ancient people who were ignorant of many things and more prone to invent fantasies than to attain scientific understanding. But, amazingly enough, these ancient people managed to discover rules well worth following if one wants to live in a supportive and peaceful community. The rules have paid off and they have brought the Cavenians into a praiseworthy lifestyle, despite the fact that they arise out of a primitive ignorance. The teachings are "true" in the sense that they recommend the same sort of lifestyle that would be recommended by a more accurate understanding of humans and the world. The teachings effectively promote a lifestyle that we find praiseworthy on independent, more knowledgeable grounds. And, so far as the teachings do this, we admire them.

Let us add one last feature to this story. Suppose we meet an intelligent young Cavenian who wants to express all this to his fellow citizens, that is, he wants to explain to them their own beliefs about the cave, and the usefulness of their own beliefs, from the perspective of a detached, rational outsider. He wants to convince them that there is nothing to fear in gaining a detached and rational understanding through science, psychology and history. Of course, it will turn out on his account that many of the Cavenian teachings and stories will be revealed to be untenable artefacts from ages long past. But, he insists, the moral *substance* of those stories and teachings will remain undisturbed, since the moral teachings of the cave are in fact quite sound and sensible. In short, he wants to convince his fellow citizens that even if the cave's teachings are nothing but myth, they can be known as such without endangering the wholesome fruits of their civilization. This bright young Cavenian, let us suppose, has a plan to publish these ideas, and he wants to know whether we think this is a good idea.

If we are at all sympathetic to him, and if we ourselves know anything about human beings, our reply should be that *he should tread most carefully.*

OUR OWN CAVE

It is not hard to see where this parable is pointing, of course. The Cavenians' devotion to their cave-scratchings mirrors the Western world's devotion to the Bible. And, as with the Cavenians, our religious devotion does not fit easily with our scientific understanding of humans and the world; nor does it square with our understanding of anthropology and history, and the tendencies of ancient peoples to invent myths as they try to explain the world.[1] Our attachment to the Bible seems to be a stubborn ideological relic from our primitive past, just as we would understand the Cavenians' attachment to be.

Indeed, modern scholarship of the Bible supports the opinion of Spinoza's that prefaces Chapter 1: that "the word of God is erroneous, mutilated, corrupt and inconsistent, [and] we have only fragments of it". The broad consensus among careful scholars is that the Bible is a haphazard compilation of works from several different sources, coming from different places and times, and with different agendas. We see multiple presentations of the same story, sometimes with a change in characters and setting, and many of the great stories of scripture seem to have been meant originally only as *aetiological myths*, that is, stories invented to explain how a certain place got its name, or why there exists a rivalry between groups, or how a common phrase came about. Early interpreters of the Bible then provided layer upon layer of interpretation on the text until the whole work came to have a sense of its own, a sense utterly divorced from the original ones its various writers intended. The Bible, frankly, is a textual mess, and we shall never get an entirely clear picture of all of the ingredients that went into its making.[2]

But – for all that – we could also point out that the teachings that emerge from the Bible, like those from the cave, on the whole recommend a sensible and wholesome lifestyle. Love your neighbour as yourself, and love the Creator above all else; do not kill, murder, steal or cheat; do justice, love mercy and walk with humility; and so on. There are many other injunctions we wonder about and should argue over, to be sure, but it is not any oversimplification to insist that the main thrust of biblical teachings, as it has come to be understood through the ages, is commendable, in light of what we know about ourselves and one another. A person living in accordance with the core teachings of the Bible seems to be a person living a life that is in no obvious way unhealthy or foolish (setting aside for now the critique Nietzsche will bring to bear on Christian morality). It would not be surprising to discover – through some branch of evolutionary biology, perhaps – that a community that followed the Bible's core teaching would fare well in competition against other societies organized around principles in conflict with the Bible's core moral teachings. Certainly a society that recommended harming one's neighbour, stealing, murdering and general dishonesty would have a hard time maintaining itself. But at the same time, no believer in the Bible would want to be told that this (alleged) evolutionary advantage is the *main* reason for wanting to live in accordance with the Bible's teaching. No, the principal virtue of such a life is its *piety*, or its expression of one's devotion to God. For the believer, that is a good thing, regardless of its worldly pay-offs.

In at least one way, the situation of the Cavenians is better than ours in relation to the Bible. They have the original writings – scratched into stone, no less! – so they do not have to deal with lost manuscripts and with the corruptions that inevitably creep into texts that are copied and passed along from generation to generation. We have not divulged any details pertaining to the original language of the scratchings, so we do not know what sort of ambiguities it has, but it is difficult to imagine any functional language that is *more* ambiguous than ancient written Hebrew. With regard to the (human) authorship, the circumstances under which the texts were created, and what other sources they drew on, we and the Cavenians are pretty much in the same position: totally in the dark.

Yet many citizens of industrial nations continue to revere the Bible, and not merely as a fascinating ancient text that manages to give good advice about living. Take the population of the United States, for example. As of 2007, almost one third of all Americans believed the Bible is "the actual word of God, to be taken literally". Nearly half agree to a weaker claim, that the Bible is "inspired" by God. And only about a fifth see it as a purely human record of ancient history, fables and legends (see Newport 2007). So there really can exist an advanced civilization – one with broad public education, that is a well-functioning democracy with very little censorship, and with only the mildest official endorsement of any religious ideas – with a heavy portion of its populace still believing that an ancient text is, in fact, a relevant, spiritually authoritative message from a transcendent being. That fact is striking, and perhaps more than anything else illustrates our puzzling, composite nature as human beings: we are capable of simultaneously upholding Enlightenment ideals alongside Iron Age superstitions. We surely are no less puzzling than the Cavenians.

Yet those of us who champion reason, and who loftily dismiss the Bible as mere superstition, should not be quite so smug. For the civilization we live and work within, and rely on for our security and survival, has a long history; and almost all of it, moral notions included, is built around that old text. All of the "compass points" of our culture lead out from it: it gives us our north, south, east and west. As Voltaire once said, "If God did not exist, it would be necessary to invent him".[3] Who is willing to predict the consequences of tearing it out from the fabric of our culture, or (which amounts to the same thing) devaluing it as mere superstition? Nietzsche was willing to do so, and what he predicted will happen when the old moral superstitions are abandoned was both thrilling and dangerous:

> The dangerous and uncanny point has been reached when the greatest, most diverse, most comprehensive life *lives past* the old morality. The "individual" is left standing there, forced to give himself laws, forced to rely on his own arts and wiles of self-preservation, self-enhancement, self-redemption. ... Danger has returned, the mother of morals, great danger, displaced onto the individual this time, onto the neighbor or friend, onto the street, onto your own child, onto your own heart, onto all your own-most, secret-most wishes and wills.   (Nietzsche [1886] 2002: 159)

That all is a *good* thing, according to Nietzsche. But many of us are (as he well knew) both timid and mediocre, and unwilling to lose the safety rails our culture places around itself.[4] We worry over what happens when individuals are forced to give themselves laws. Will they prescribe the golden rule to themselves? Or will it be laws of greed and tyranny? That is not a silly worry to have. It is one thing to put your own wishes and wills on the line; it is quite another to put your children and loved ones on the line. Do we really trust that we will give ourselves *good* laws? Do we trust *everyone* to do so? Do we dare to live apart from the superstitions that have brought us safe this far?

THAT YOUNG MAN: SPINOZA

Like the young Cavenian who wants to tell the Cavenians that their religion is a kind of beneficial myth, Spinoza's goal was to show the Bible to be a beneficial myth, along with the assurance that we would not endanger ourselves or our civilization by admitting such a thing. But Spinoza also tried to demonstrate something more surprising: *that the Bible itself, interpreted properly, does not present itself as anything other than a guide to moral behaviour that is rooted in various kinds of illusions.* The Bible "knows", so to speak, that its moral commandments are not based on accurate knowledge, although it insists at the same time that they ought to be obeyed anyway. Those interpreters of the Bible who claim that it is infallible on all matters, or that it reliably offers an accurate understanding of the world, or was written under the direct guidance of an omniscient deity, just are not reading it carefully enough.

Spinoza published his *Theological-Political Treatise* in order to demonstrate this, and to argue that a republic interested in longevity and stability would do well to enforce the basic morality revealed by scripture: and to let its citizenry make up their own minds about everything else. Invoking the classical authority of Tacitus, he reminded his readers that those times are happiest when one can think as one pleases and say what one thinks. For, so long as everyone is following basic moral precepts, what they are saying and thinking should not matter that much; moreover, we all shall be happier being able to say what we believe than if we have to try to censor minds and tongues. A stable and enduring republic, Spinoza argued, will allow the freedom to philosophize.

Had Spinoza been successful in convincing his neighbours and his government of this, he then would have had the opportunity to share with them his own metaphysics. Of course, the *Theological-Political Treatise* was not well received; one early reviewer characterized it as "a book forged in hell", and for centuries Spinozism was viewed as a philosophy to react against.[5] Spinoza resigned himself to a posthumous publication of his masterpiece, the *Ethics*.

A TRUE PORTRAIT OF GOD

In the *Ethics*, Spinoza argued for a proper conception of God, one that grows from sound reasoning and philosophical principles, and not from Iron Age superstitions and rank anthropomorphism. We shall examine this conception in greater depth in the following chapters, but a brief overview can be given here.

The core of our concept of God is of an entity that provides a basis for all explanation. There must be something that explains why the world is and why the world has the nature it has. If this explanation is to be genuine, none of the answers can be the least bit arbitrary. God must be of such a nature that, in knowing God, one can ask no further questions. So God, for Spinoza, must be a substance whose existence is necessary and whose pure nature determines all that exists. There can be no substance genuinely distinct from God; for then that substance would be a further, separate thing to explain. Everything is God or is rooted in God. Or, as Spinoza demonstrates early on, "Whatever is, is in God, and nothing can be or be conceived without God" (*Ethics* IP15).

This means that everything in the world is rooted in God's own necessary nature (for otherwise, again, something would be left unexplained). So all that is and all that happens are necessary, and there is no way anything can be otherwise. We believe things can be otherwise, of course, but that is only because we do not see the big picture. As we understand ourselves and the things around us, we can begin to see the necessity and the relation of all things to the one God. As we gain this understanding, and see ourselves as rooted in God, our minds will fill with the satisfaction of insight, and we shall bear with greater patience and equanimity the burdens and obstacles thrown at our lives. With a sound under-standing of nature and human nature we shall do what we can to make lives smoother and open greater access to insight. When we die, we shall do so with the recognition that the very substance of our lives, the source of all being, will remain as unchanged as ever, and we shall gain some solace in that.

Spinoza knew that God, properly conceived, could not be the sort of person described in the Bible. Indeed, such an infinite, nec-essary and changeless substance cannot be a person at all. God cannot be prayed to, or feared, or loved in the way we might love another person. This conception of God is obviously opposed to the one we find among believers today, and this certainly was also true in Spinoza's day. But Spinoza's primary efforts in both the *Theological-Political Treatise* and the *Ethics* were to show that the conception is not as impossible, not as "unlivable", as we might ini-tially believe. He believed it was time for us to step beyond our primitive mythologies and live with a conception of God that could be rooted in reason. Indeed, he believed the God he was describing was the very same God as seen by the ancient prophets, although their understanding was not as clear as the one now available to us. As Spinoza might well ask: what should stop us now from believing what we know must be true?

1

Reading scripture rightly

Those who consider the Bible in its current state a letter from God, sent from heaven to men, will undoubtedly protest that I have sinned "against the Holy Ghost" by claiming the word of God is erroneous, mutilated, corrupt and inconsistent, that we have only fragments of it, and that the original text of the covenant which God made with the Jews has perished.   (*Theological-Political* 12.1)

[M]y intellect does not extend so far as to embrace all the means God possesses for bringing men to the love of himself, that is, to salvation.   (*Letters* 21, to Blijenburgh)

CONTROVERSIES IN INTERPRETATION

Spinoza published his *Theological-Political Treatise* (1670) in the midst of a controversy over how the Bible is to be interpreted: a controversy that seems to be present in just about every age. The basic tension is always between what the Bible seems to say, at least on its surface, and the various sets of doctrines and beliefs we want to see in it. The two are usually quite different. Broad traditions within Judaism and Christianity understand God to be an infinite, perfect and eternal being, omniscient and omnipotent and perfectly benevolent. Reason itself, it has seemed, even requires this view of a perfect being. But the Bible only occasionally supports such an idea. The same traditions have wanted to see the Bible as coherent, factually accurate and as relevant to our age as to any other; yet the Bible itself seems reluctant to meet this wish, and presents itself as an untamed jungle, with no shortage of puzzles and paradoxes that reason is unable to penetrate. So various strategies of interpretation have developed over time, offering different ways to resolve this basic tension between scripture and reason.

Two possible broad strategies emerge in response to this tension: one can find ways to read the truths of reason into scripture ("biblical rationalism", so to speak), or one can prefer what scripture says to what reason demands ("biblical literalism"). Both strategies were represented in the controversy as it surfaced in Spinoza's time.

On the one hand, there was Lodewijk Meijer, a friend of Spinoza's, who represented biblical rationalism. In his *Philosophy as the Interpreter of Holy Scripture* ([1666] 2005), Meijer argued that in order to get at the true sense of the Bible, we must find the genuine truth hidden in the Bible. In order to do this, we must first know, through science and philosophy, what is clearly and distinctly known to be true; and then we must find ways to interpret the Bible so that it reflects this knowledge. Now someone might object that this seems more like misinterpreting the Bible than interpreting it correctly. But Meijer had a clever answer to this objection. He reasoned that God would be able to foresee all of the possible ways in which humans might interpret or misinterpret scripture. Moreover, God would also foresee all of the interpretive difficulties we were bound to face, as humans learned more about the natural world and discovered apparent conflicts between what the Bible seems to tell us about the world and what reason tells us about it. (For example, the Bible tells us Joshua commanded the sun to stand still, yet modern science tells us it is the earth and not the sun that moves, and so on.) Since we are rational creatures, it is natural for us to try to find new ways of interpreting scripture, ways that allow us to square it with what reason teaches. (So we interpret Joshua's command as really being a command for the earth to stop revolving.) God would foresee all this as well, of course, so we reach Meijer's intended conclusion: that the *intended* meaning of scripture – God's own authorial intent behind the work – is the interpretation that we shall construct as we try to square scripture with what reason teaches. God *intended* for us to use our reason in obtaining the right interpretation of scripture; reading the truth as reason teaches it into scripture gets us to the intended meaning of scripture.

Meijer's conclusion was, at the same time, an ingenious attempt to preserve the widespread conviction that the Bible must be true with a very real and pressing need to find some principled way of adjudicating among competing interpretations of scripture. As the old Dutch saying has it, *elke ketter heeft zijn letter* (every heretic has his text), and there never has been a shortage of impassioned readers finding passages to oppose one another's interpretation of scripture. But what reason teaches us, Meijer believed, must be univocal; we never will discover both a claim and its contradictory to be true. Thus reason provides a neutral ground for sorting out which interpretation is correct, and can put to rest the endless wrangling over passages and how to interpret them.

But the wrangling, of course, was not put to rest. The following year, Petrus Serrarius responded to Meijer from a stance that prized scripture, as interpreted through the Holy Spirit, over the truths known by reason. Serrarius was sceptical both of the power of reason to unlock the meaning of scripture and of the legitimacy of religious institutions. He believed our best course is to pray as individuals for God's guidance and inspiration, and patiently await the second coming (which he had predicted would come in December 1662; see Fix 1990: 72–7, 106–8). In his 1667 response to Meijer, Serrarius argued that it must be the Holy Spirit, and not reason, that decides our interpretations of scripture. He could profitably enlist Paul as an authority advocating the same position:

> For what person knows a man's thoughts except the spirit of the man which is in him? So also no one comprehends the thoughts of God except the Spirit of God. Now we have received not the spirit of the world, but the Spirit which is from God, that we might understand the gifts bestowed on us by God. (1 Cor. 2:11–13)

It is the Spirit that guided the hands of scripture's ancient authors, and thus the same Spirit is required for us to understand what was intended. Reason, or human wisdom, has nothing to offer.

One of Serrarius's motivating worries is easy to appreciate. If, as Meijer had argued, natural knowledge and reason give us all the guidance we need to interpret scripture, then why exactly does anyone need scripture? Why not simply live by reason? If scripture has any value at all, it must be because there are some important truths that cannot be known through reason, and can be known only through some supernatural agency or avenue such as the Holy Spirit. Reason must be insufficient.

Several other books contributed to the controversy. Louis Wolzogen argued in 1668 for a middle way, which urged that natural knowledge or reason should guide our interpretations (when that knowledge was beyond all doubt), but it should not be allowed to touch the central mysteries of Christianity, which must be revealed to us by the Holy Spirit (see Israel 2001: 205–8). Samuel Maresius argued in 1670 that the Cartesian philosophers of the day (such as Meijer) were making difficulties where in fact there were none. The true interpretation of scripture is on its surface, and is accessed easily and naturally (see Preus 2009: ch. 3; see also Israel 2001: 209–12). (So long, we may be tempted to add, as one does not probe very deeply or think too long about it.)

So Spinoza entered into the fray in 1670 with his *Theological-Political Treatise*. As we shall see, his view was in some ways a compromise. He agreed with Meijer that, at least on the core issues, scripture and reason were indeed in harmony with one another (although Spinoza certainly did not approve of Meijer's method of interpretation).[1] And he agreed with Serrarius that reason cannot offer everything scripture provides (although he certainly did not share Serrarius's scepticism towards reason). But this "compromise", of course, was not in any way a peaceful settlement of the controversy. Indeed, it initiated another controversy large enough to eclipse the earlier one entirely.

According to Spinoza, what we shall find when we study scripture *carefully* is that it is far less magical and other-worldly than is commonly supposed. We may think initially that it is full of stories of humans communicating with God and impossible miracles.

But in fact, Spinoza claims, it is not. The Bible is instead a work that is very open about the fallibility of its prophets and the perfect ordinariness of its so-called miracles. The Bible, in fact, does not present itself as anything other than a set of recommendations about how one should believe and behave if one does not have accurate knowledge of the natural world around them. Spinoza, like the young Cavenian, thinks we can recognize this without losing any of our esteem for this ancient work.

To understand how he makes his case, we shall examine his discussions of prophets, miracles and scripture's moral teachings. Then, from these discussions, we shall assemble a more general account of Spinoza's attitude towards scripture.

PROPHECY, SPINOZA STYLE

Prophecy, according to Spinoza, is "certain knowledge about something revealed to men by God" (*Theological-Political* 1.1). He immediately notes that, under this definition, natural knowledge could also be understood as prophecy, since "what we know by the natural light of reason depends on knowledge of God and his eternal decrees alone" (*Theological-Political* 1.2). Indeed, Spinoza argues that natural knowledge has as much right to be called "divine" as any other kind of knowledge, since all the natural truths about the world are ultimately grounded in God's nature and God's decrees. But, of course, most people mean something else when they talk about "prophecy" and "prophets", so Spinoza turns to the knowledge humans might gain through avenues other than the natural light of reason. More specifically, he turns to the way in which the Bible talks about such non-natural knowledge.

What he finds, he claims, is that in every instance of prophecy described in the Bible, the prophets in question never are given truths directly from God (except for Christ – a special case we shall discuss shortly). Instead, the truths are revealed to the prophets always through words or images, either privately (when the prophet is in some kind of dream or "vision" state) or publicly (in such a way as to also be observable by other people). In neither of these cases can it be said that God is communicating *directly* with the prophets; he communicates only through the mediation of some created thing.

Consider first the prophecies that come in dreams and visions. Abimelech (Gen. 20.6) and Joseph (Gen. 5–11) are explicitly said to have received God's instructions while dreaming. David (1 Chron. 21:16), Balaam (Num. 22:22–34), Joshua (Josh. 5:13–15), and Isaiah (Isa. 6) all experienced visions of God or of God's angels. Only Moses, Spinoza argues, heard a real voice; and he deduces from Deuteronomy 34.10 ("And there has not arisen a prophet since in Israel like Moses, whom the Lord knew face to face") that every prophet after Moses must have encountered God only through dreams or visions. These "visions", Spinoza explains, are thoroughly *imaginative*, meaning that they engage the imaginative capacities of the prophets, which means that they might not reflect anything real in the physical world. Imaginative visions, whether divine or mundane in content, can easily be hallucinations or misperceptions. Furthermore, if we agree with traditional theology and Spinoza's own metaphysics that God is not any sort of finite corporeal body, we know that any "vision" of God must not be really a veridical perception of God. God is not the sort of being that can be seen, or even heard, in any normal way. Any vision must then be, at most, an imaginative idea meant to somehow represent God.

Traditional interpreters of the Bible would agree, in a way, with this account. But, of course, they would add that the dreams or visions experienced by the prophets had *God* as their cause, and not the sort of ordinary causes that typically bring about dreams and hallucinations. But here Spinoza agrees in return:

> I confess that I do not know by what natural laws prophetic insight occurred. I might, like others, have said that it occurred by the power of God, but then I would be saying nothing meaningful. … For everything is done by the power of God. Indeed, because the power of nature is nothing other than the power of God itself, it is certain that we fail to understand the power of God to the extent that we are ignorant of natural causes.
>
> (*Theological-Political* 1.27)

16

So Spinoza agrees that the prophetic visions are caused by God, but insists that this is no different, in the end, from saying that they are brought about by natural causes. He confesses that he is in no position to present any account of those causes (presumably because we do not have enough of an account of the details in each circumstance), but he is confident that there is, in each case, a natural explanation. This is surely not something most traditional theists would accept; we shall see Spinoza's defence of his claim next, when we turn to his account of miracles.

Now Spinoza also claims that, at least in some instances, God communicates to prophets in public ways, that is, ways that are not purely private mental experiences, as dreams and hallucinations are, but could be shared by more than one observer. His central example is God's communication of the Ten Commandments to Moses, which he thinks is best understood as a case where God communicated with Moses with a real voice, "that is, in the manner in which two men normally communicate their thoughts to each other by means of their two bodies" (*Theological-Political* 1.11).[2] So this is not a case in which some dream or vision fails to correspond to reality; the experience is veridical. And this makes the case especially puzzling to Spinoza:

> For it seems quite contrary to reason to assert that a created thing [such as a voice] depending upon God in the same way as other created things, could express or explain in its own person the essence or existence of God in fact or words, that is, by declaring in the first person, "I am Jehovah your God", etc.   (*Theological-Political* 1.12)

Spinoza's puzzlement is over why anyone would take a created thing, mouthing such words, to be an instrument being employed by an infinite, eternal, changeless being. We might wonder: if a man, donkey, or pillar of fire were to declare to us "I am the number seventeen", how could we possibly relate that voice to that number? The number is not a man or a donkey, or indeed any sort of thing that can manipulate a body into speaking its mind; but neither, according to Spinoza, is God. So why would a human ever take a humanlike voice as issuing either directly or indirectly from an eternal, infinite being?

Spinoza appears to suggest one solution to this puzzle a couple of pages later. He observes that Moses's "face-to-face" relation to God might say more about Moses's own attitude towards the voice he hears than it does about Moses's interaction with God. Being "face to face" with God could mean simply that the Lord "speaks with me as a friend, not as one who is terrified" (*Theological-Political* 1.17).[3] If so, then Moses is "face to face" with God in the sense that his experienced encounter with God does not terrify him. This opens the door to construing Moses's experience as merely a dream or vision, unique only in that Moses did not find the experience terrifying. But Spinoza then goes on to reject this answer to the puzzle, and returns to the assertion that Moses and God interacted in just the way two humans do when they have a conversation. He notes along the way that in the case of a prophet with a "vastly superior" mind – like Christ – the communication between God and prophet is immediate. Christ received his revelations not through words or images, but directly; "and that is why [we can say that] God revealed himself to the Apostles through the mind of Christ, as he did, formerly, to Moses by means of a heavenly voice. Therefore the voice of Christ may be called the voice of God, like the voice which Moses heard" (*Theological-Political* 1.18). He concludes that "if Moses spoke with God face to face as a man with his friend (that is, through the mediation of two bodies), Christ communicated with God from mind to mind" (*Theological-Political* 1.19). This seems to reassert that Moses's "face-to-face" experience was not a dream or merely subjective vision.

What are we to make of this discussion? Does Spinoza think Moses heard a real voice or not? If so, then how does he solve the puzzle of how an eternal God can speak through creatures? If not, then why does he seem to return to that conclusion? The answer could simply be that Spinoza is only trying to interpret the sense of the Bible, and not defend its truth. He does profess that "What I have just said, I infer from Scripture" (*Theological-Political* 1.19), and he seems to put some distance between his own beliefs and what he has inferred. Thus he may be simply asserting that, usually, the Bible makes it clear that the prophets are dreaming or experiencing non-veridical "visions", but in the case of Moses, scripture plainly intends to say that he heard a real voice, although we really do not have any way of understanding how this could be so.

An alternative answer is one that Spinoza may have been hinting at slyly, between the lines. He suggests to us that Moses's "face-to-face" relation to God was like a man's relation to a friend; and we know that the voice of someone (like Christ) whose mind is directly "in tune" with God's mind may be called the voice of God. So perhaps we should infer that when Moses heard God's voice, he really was only hearing the real (and not merely imagined) voice of a friend. This is a highly speculative reading, to be sure, and it runs against Spinoza's claim that no one other than Christ had the direct connection to God he describes, since that would leave out any such enlightened friend of Moses. But, in its favour, the reading would explain why Spinoza suddenly inserts a discussion of Christ in the middle of such a confusing account of Moses.

In any case, Spinoza's overall conclusion regarding the scripture's account of prophecy is clear: "apart from Christ, no one has received revelations from God except by means of the imagination, namely by words or visions, and therefore prophecy does not require a more perfect mind but a more vivid imagination" (*Theological-Political* 1.20). In other words, the Bible itself does not portray the prophets as anything other than humans with average minds and very active imaginations. Let me underscore this point once more: *the Bible, according to Spinoza, does not mean to suggest that the prophets are anything more than men whose imaginations often outrun their reason.*

MIRACLES, SPINOZA-STYLE

In chapter 6 of the *Theological-Political Treatise*, Spinoza criticizes common beliefs about miracles. The traditional view, as Spinoza describes it, is that "God is inactive whilst nature follows its normal course", but occasionally God actively disrupts that normal course and brings about an event that can be explained only by God's superior power (*Theological-Political* 6.1). Thus there are two powers – nature's and God's – and nature rules while God is inactive, but is rendered superfluous by God's sudden action.

Such a view is incoherent, Spinoza will argue, and moreover does not agree with scripture. His argument for the incoherence of miracles can be summarized as follows (taken from *Theological-Political* 6.2–6.3):

1. God's understanding is not distinct from God's will; that is, what God understands, God wills, and what God wills, God understands.
2. God wills the universal laws of nature to be true.
3. Hence, God understands the universal laws of nature to be true.
4. Any event that contradicted the laws of nature would be an event God could neither will not understand.
5. What God neither wills nor understands cannot exist.
6. Hence, miracles cannot exist.

The key notion is that one cannot simultaneously hold that the laws of nature are decreed by God and that exceptions to those laws are also decreed by God, because that would mean that God wills a contradiction. In response, a traditional theist might insist that God decrees not the universal laws of nature but instead those laws with "special occasions" tagged for their suspension. Leibniz provided this kind of response, distinguishing between God's "subordinate maxims" (or laws of nature) and God's "general will", which include events that violate those subordinate maxims but do not violate the most comprehensive decrees God made in the creation of the world (*Discourse on Metaphysics*, §7; Leibniz [1675–1716] 1989: 40). God, in short, decrees general laws along with a set of exceptions to them.

Spinoza does not countenance such a response explicitly, but he does provide a further argument that might be used in reply. He argues that miracles cannot be conceived as issuing from God's essence or existence: that, in other words, a miracle would in no way demonstrate anything about God. The argument is as follows (*Theological-Political* 6.6):

1. If God's existence is not known through itself, it must be deduced "from concepts whose truth is so firm and unques-

tionable that no power capable of changing them can exist, or be conceived".

2. Everything that can be known and understood in nature must also conform to these firm and unquestionable concepts.
3. If we try to conceive an event in nature that does not so conform, then either (a) we are trying to conceive something that is absurd, or (b) we must doubt the "firm and unquestionable" concepts.
4. If (b), then we also doubt the existence of God.
5. Neither (a) nor (b) can count as anything other than diminishment of our knowledge of God's essence or existence.
6. Hence, "we cannot infer from miracles either the essence or existence, or the providence, of God, but on the contrary these are far better inferred from the fixed and immutable order of nature".

This argument is different from the first, since it appeals to the "firm and unquestionable concepts" that provide justification both for belief in God and for the laws of nature. Basically, by admitting miracles, one rejects the stable set of concepts that also justify our knowledge of God's essence and existence. This can be applied to the Leibnizian reply seen above in the following general way: in so far as our belief in God rests on exceptionless axioms or truths, any events defined as exceptions to those truths will inevitably cause us to doubt the existence of God. Thus, believing that God wills exceptions to the laws of nature (or exceptions to Leibniz's "subordinate maxims") should weaken our faith in the exceptionless claims that ground our belief in God, for why couldn't these "exceptionless" claims also have exceptions? That is not the end of the debate, to be sure, since Leibniz has plenty more ammunition in his metaphysical armoury, but it is perhaps enough to show that there is real tension between belief in a god whose existence is meant to be provable from exceptionless *a priori* principles and belief in a god who decrees exceptions to universal laws.

So Spinoza argues, on metaphysical grounds, that miracles really do not "fit" with God's nature. But – and this is the surprise – he also believes he can argue for the same conclusion on scriptural grounds. He cites Psalm 148, which urges the sun and moon, the shining stars, the highest heavens, and the waters above the heavens all to praise the Lord: "For he commanded and they were created. / And he established them for ever and ever; / He fixed their bounds which cannot be passed". He cites also a passage in Jeremiah, and several from "the philosopher" of Ecclesiastes. What is interesting here is not really how compellingly these passages support Spinoza's conclusion (for they are poetic expressions, and not very compelling as support for a philosophical claim), but rather Spinoza's bold claim that *scripture itself is opposed to using miracles as any evidence for God's existence.* That should come to many readers of scripture as something of a surprise.

Spinoza also argues in this chapter that the alleged "miracles" of the Bible are best understood as events that, according to scripture's authors, were perfectly natural occurrences but poorly understood by the people at the time. In the accounts of a great many of these events, we also find descriptions of concomitant events that may have served as partial causes. For example, Moses has to throw ashes up into the air in order for the Egyptians to be afflicted with boils (Exod. 9:10); a wind has to blow all night in order to part the Red Sea (Exod. 14:21); and Elisha has to lay atop a boy all night in order to warm him and resuscitate him (2 Kings 4:34). Other allegedly miraculous events are perfectly natural themselves: thus Samuel met Saul by happenstance, Noah saw a rainbow and the Pharoah failed to feel compassion (that is, his "heart hardened"). And so on, until Spinoza is confident enough to conclude that "all things that are truly reported to have happened in Scripture necessarily happened according to the laws of nature, as all things do" (*Theological-Political* 6.15). Indeed, Spinoza is so confident that scripture never intends to say that events have happened contrary to the laws of nature that he believes we can rule out any scriptural claim to the contrary as something inserted later by no-good interpolators:

> If anything is found which can be demonstrated conclusively to contradict the laws of nature or which could not possibly [be understood] to follow from them, we must accept in every case that it was interpolated into the Bible by blasphemous persons. For whatever is contrary

to nature, is contrary to reason, and what is contrary to reason, is absurd, and accordingly to be rejected.

(*Theological-Political* 6.15)

That is some confidence. Miracles, Spinoza claims, so obviously contradict theism that any insistence on them is blasphemous. Attributing a miracle to God is like accusing God of committing an "unnatural" act.

SCRIPTURE'S MORAL FOCUS

But in a sense these discussions about prophecy and miracles are beside the point, since scripture, according to Spinoza, does not aim at providing special knowledge of the nature of God or of metaphysics. Scripture's main intent, he claims, is to promote a moral lifestyle, motivated by a few basic attitudes. The "basis and foundation of the whole of Scripture", according to Spinoza, is "That there is a God, one and omnipotent, who alone is to be adored and cares for all men, loving most those who worship Him and love their neighbour as themselves, etc." (*Theological-Political* 7.6).

As a brief, one-sentence synopsis of the Bible, that is not bad. The core of the Bible is a recommendation to love one's neighbour and love God above all else, and that the obedient will win favour. Spinoza's key interpretive move is based on this recognition, as his recommendation is to interpret the whole of scripture in the light of this overarching theme. The Bible should be read and understood to aim consistently at this broad conclusion, and other matters raised by scripture can be either settled or set aside as our idle curiosities dictate. (Similarly, anyone who tries to learn ancient history or Mediterranean geography from Homer's *Odyssey* should not lose sight of the fact that the work's principal aim is not to record these things, but to entertain, inspire and be brought into culture.)

Indeed, Spinoza argues that scripture is explicit that "an intellectual or precise knowledge of God" is not generally available to everyone, and is not required in order to be obedient to scripture's injunctions. God tells Moses (Exod. 6:3) that he was revealed to

Abraham, Isaac and Jacob not by his name "Jehovah", but as El Shaddai, meaning "God who suffices". God was also called simply "El" or "Eloha", meaning "the Powerful", or alternatively "the Great", "the Terrible", "the Just" and so on: or all of them put together at once in the plural. Hence, concludes Spinoza, the patriarchs "knew no attribute of God disclosing his absolute essence, but only his acts and promises" (*Theological-Political* 13.5), that is, the important thing was not who or what God really is, or even God's true name, but what God does or will do so far as human beings are concerned. Thus "people are not obliged by commandment to know God's attributes" (*Theological-Political* 13.5). They are obliged only to know of God what is required in order to move them toward obedience to God's commandments.

Spinoza argues furthermore that, according to the experience of Jeremiah, Moses and John, what humans are obliged to know about God is that God is supremely just and merciful; no further knowledge of God is required (*Theological-Political* 13.8). Spinoza's conclusion from this discussion is, as usual, both bold and surprising:

> From all this, we conclude that intellectual knowledge of God, considering His nature as it is in itself, a nature which men cannot emulate by a certain rationale of living and cannot adopt as a paradigm for cultivating a true rationale for living, has no relevance whatsoever to faith and revealed religion, and consequently *men may have totally the wrong ideas about God's nature without doing any wrong.* (*Theological-Political* 13.8; emphasis added)

Once again, Spinoza does not take this to be merely his own view; he takes this to be the explicit conclusion of scripture. One need not really know God's nature at all in order to do right by God. In fact, as Spinoza hints with a nod towards what the *Ethics* will teach in detail, God's true nature could not possibly serve as any sort of exemplar for lives humans can live.

Spinoza later provides "the dogmas of universal faith", or the basic beliefs about God scripture teaches consistently throughout its many books. These are beliefs that are required in order to motivate a pious lifestyle:

1. There is a God who is supremely just and merciful, or an exemplar of the true life, who should be acknowledged and obeyed as like a judge.
2. God is one and alone, which is a required belief for supreme devotion, admiration and love.
3. God is present everywhere, and is aware of all things.
4. God has power over all things, and is obliged by no one.
5. Worshipping God consists in justice and charity, or in love of one's neighbour.
6. All and only those who worship and obey God are saved.
7. God forgives all those who repent of their sins.

There is often discussion among scholars over whether Spinoza can possibly believe any of these tenets, even in some metaphorical way, since they all seem to suggest or rely on an anthropomorphic conception of God (as lawgiver, judge, king, etc.). But the discussions miss an obvious point. Spinoza has just argued that people do not need an accurate conception of God in order to be pious; what they need is the characterization as given by these tenets. And with each tenet Spinoza suggests why people need that particular belief in order to be moved to obedience. For example, with the last one, Spinoza writes, "if this were not clearly established, all would despair of their salvation ... But anyone who believes that God forgives ... is more fully inspired with the love of God" (*Theological-Political* 14.10).

The dogmas of universal faith are clearly oriented toward getting people to behave in a certain way (see further Curley 2010: 24–7). Believe that there is an all-powerful, all-knowing being who expects you to act with justice and mercy in all your dealings; know that, when you do fail, this being will forgive you and give you a second chance; know that you will be "saved" (whatever that means) only if you strive to please this being. It is an effective set of beliefs to inspire moral living. And that, according to Spinoza, is all that scripture tries to provide, and all that it has ever meant to provide: "For the aim of philosophy is nothing but truth, but the aim of faith, as we have abundantly demonstrated, is simply obedience and piety" (*Theological-Political* 14.13).

INTERPRETING SCRIPTURE, SPINOZA STYLE

Having seen Spinoza's treatment of prophets and miracles, and his account of scripture's core of moral teaching, we are in a position to understand his general recommendations for interpreting scripture. From what we have seen, Spinoza is committed to the following three interpretive principles:

1. Interpretations of passages should be as naturalistic as the text allows.
2. Attach significance to passages to the extent that they express scripture's core moral teaching.
3. Reject recalcitrant passages or interpretations as somehow corrupted.

This set of principles might not appear to match how Spinoza characterizes his own method for interpreting scripture, which is "to claim nothing as a biblical doctrine that we have not derived, by the closest possible scrutiny, from its own [i.e. the Bible's] history" (*Theological-Political* 7.5). But on closer analysis, as I shall explain, the two amount to the same thing (at least in Spinoza's hands).

Spinoza's first injunction, in recounting his method for interpretation, is to know as much as possible about "the history of Scripture" (*Theological-Political* 7.5). This means, first, knowing the original language of the texts, in all its subtleties and idioms. It means, second, building a lexicon about everything scripture has to say about all the topics it raises. Here it is especially important not to read what we take to be the truth into scripture, but to try to grasp what scripture means to say, on the whole or for the most part, about each topic. Finally, we need to know, as thoroughly as possible, the circumstances in which the various texts were written, who their authors were and what their psychological temperaments were; and we also need to know how the texts were handed down through time, how they came to be included in the Bible and so on.

This first "historical" stage amounts to the same thing as interpreting scripture as naturalistically as possible. For as Spinoza deploys his lexicon of scripture – think now of his extensive examinations of prophecy and miracles – his interpretations are about as naturalistic as possible. Aided by insights about the psychological temperaments of the original authors and audiences, Spinoza finds his way to the conclusion that, according to scripture itself, the prophets were for the most part extraordinarily imaginative social activists, and no events recorded in the Bible were meant to be described as having violated the laws of nature (although the ignorant people at the time may not have been able to provide any natural explanation for those events). He also comes to the conclusion that, according to scripture itself, one need not truly know God in order to be "saved", but only believe the sorts of things about God likely to motivate one to behave piously.

Spinoza's second stage in interpreting scripture is to cautiously gather up what seem to be scripture's "universal doctrine", that is, what scripture consistently teaches throughout its various parts, in an analogy to the fact that nature has patterns and laws found consistently through its various parts (*Theological-Political* 7.6). It is here that we shall find the "dogmas of universal faith" and scripture's moral core. Once we uncover this, Spinoza says, then we can turn to less universal and more puzzling things, and:

> Anything found in the Scriptures about these [less universal] things which is obscure and ambiguous, should be explained and decided only by the Bible's universal doctrine, and where such passages are self-contradictory [that is to say, contradict what reason teaches – CH], we must consider on what occasion, when, and to whom they were written.　　　　　(*Theological-Political* 7.7)

This second stage is crucial for allowing Spinoza to secure what he wants from scripture – namely, its practical, moral advice – while leaving behind the hopeless metaphysical baggage that cannot at all be squared with what reason teaches (or, at any rate, what the *Ethics* will teach). He can then take scripture seriously to the extent that its moral advice coincides with what reason also teaches, and discount or "explain away" other passages in scripture through knowledge of the more contingent features of their authorship.

The third interpretive principle I am attributing to Spinoza ("Reject recalcitrant passages or interpretations as somehow corrupted") allows him, of course, to discount the passages that cannot be straightforwardly naturalized and do not figure prominently in scripture's core moral teaching. But the principle does more than that. Spinoza, of course, was well aware of the fact that the interpretation he was providing was far from orthodox, and far from anything even appearing as a possibility to readers of scripture. His reading of sacred texts was like that of the young Cavenian we imagined in the introduction, who wanted to demonstrate that the cave-scratchings provided good moral advice, even if it is acknowledged that the advice comes from primitive and ignorant origins. But, unlike our young Cavenian, Spinoza went further, indeed, so far as to insist that the way in which he was reading scripture was precisely the way in which its authors intended for it to be taken. Namely, scripture is a work recounting a historic people's struggle to come to a moral code and provide motivation for following it, even motivation rooted in deep ignorance of both nature and God. This conclusion, Spinoza insists, comes straight from the most defensible reading of scripture itself.

This means that Spinoza can reject recalcitrant passages and any interpretation that would have scripture trying to establish any other conclusion. Rationalist interpretations that would have scripture giving an account of the world mirroring that given by reason and science, and more "literalistic" or fideistic interpretations requiring a supernatural "spirit" for gaining the true, intended meaning of scripture, are all to be rejected as falling foul of what "scripture itself" – its history, its lexicon, its core dogmas – plainly teaches. Spinoza is claiming not only that it is possible to "naturalize" scripture and strip it of its authority in metaphysical matters but also that other ways of interpreting scripture must be rejected as consequences of not having studied it carefully enough.

APPROPRIATING SCRIPTURE

In a recent book on the *Theological-Political Treatise*, Theo Verbeek (2003) argues that Spinoza intended the work to pave a way for the publication of the *Ethics*. In the seventeenth century, Verbeek argues, an "atheist" was understood to be someone who denies that God establishes moral laws for human behaviour in the way that a human lawmaker might. Spinoza's *Ethics* makes this denial quite explicitly, of course. So, according to Verbeek, Spinoza first had to establish that one can make this denial while at the same time affirming both the reality of God and the ultimate soundness of the Bible's moral teachings. "God-Lawgiver" can be replaced by "God-Nature" without weakening morality in the least.

But if the argument of this chapter is correct, the *Theological-Political Treatise* was meant to do even more than this. It is one thing to show that one's forthcoming philosophical work *can be made consistent with* the existing religion of one's culture; it is another to attempt to demonstrate that the religion of one's culture, when studied carefully, actually *anticipates* one's forthcoming philosophical work. It is this second claim that Spinoza was making. In Spinoza's mind, I submit, the *Ethics* lays out what the truth has always been about God, humanity and the universe, and the authors of the Bible were subject to this truth, and in some ways even grasped it, although in a far from perfect way and in only primitive terms. What they were able to grasp accurately were the practical consequences of Spinoza's theology: that happiness in this life consists in treating one's neighbour with justice and mercy, and blessedness or salvation consists in the adoration of the one perfect being. Along the way, of course, the ancient authors tended to anthropomorphize this one being and misunderstand nature, as well as their own experience; but to their great credit they knew enough to devote the centre of their attention to instilling piety and obedience in a population all too prone to violence and disorder. In doing this, they safeguarded their culture, which eventually allowed for the possibility of advanced civilization, and the flourishing of science and metaphysics, which (at last) will grant at least some of us a more accurate glimpse into the nature of nature, and the nature of the one being in whom we remain, and who remains in us.[4]

2

God, as known by reason

To your question as to whether I have as clear an idea of God as of a triangle, I reply in the affirmative. But if you ask me whether I have as clear a mental image of God as of a triangle, I reply in the negative. We cannot imagine God, but we can apprehend him by the intellect.

(*Letters* 56, to Boxel)

Do you take it for arrogance and pride that I resort to reason, and that I give my acceptance to this, the true Word of God, which is in the mind and can never be distorted or corrupted? Away with this destructive superstition, and acknowledge the faculty of reason which God gave you, and cultivate it, unless you would be counted among the beasts. (*Letters* 76, to Burgh)

THE GOD OF LOGICAL SPACE

We have seen that, in the *Theological-Political Treatise* and in the *Political Treatise*, Spinoza sought to assure his readers that the existing moral, religious and political structures of his day did not require belief in a personal divine entity interfering every now and then in human affairs. Indeed, he argued, a civil society is improved by allowing philosophers the freedom to pursue a more accurate understanding of God through reason. It is now time to turn to the details of the philosophers' more accurate understanding of God.

Every understanding of God is set against a backdrop of metaphysics. This backdrop is what makes it an understanding, as an explanation is always a broader context into which we project the phenomenon being explained. In myths, the broader context is always a story of a somewhat familiar kind, such as terrible forces at war with one another, or a cosmic parent working out a relationship with its offspring, or giant animals doing what comes naturally to them, and so on. Generally, we can learn from these mythologies what sorts of relationships were foremost on their authors' minds, as they took their innermost concerns and projected them onto the grandest possible cosmological backdrop. Creators are conceived in the image of their creatures, as Spinoza once told a correspondent: "[A] triangle, if it could speak, would likewise say that God is eminently triangular, and a circle that God's nature is eminently circular" (*Letters* 56, to Boxel).

But in a rationalistic philosophy like Spinoza's, the backdrop is decidedly less human and far less familiar. Spinoza's backdrop is *the space of logical possibilities*. Think of this space as a field whose contours are dictated by the implications of concepts, definitions and principles. Think of it as the space charted by geometers as they discover what relation shapes and lines must have to one another, or the territory of truths uncovered by mathematicians as they explore what happens once a number line is established. We might initially think of these spaces as nothing more than what we imagine them to be, as they seem to be mere abstractions or creatures of our brains. But it cannot be only a matter of imagination; for consider geometers and mathematicians, who are constantly surprised by what they find they can prove, as well as by what they find they cannot prove. No one has been able to prove whether every even number is the sum of two primes (Goldbach's conjecture), yet it seems there must be a truth to the matter, even if it turns out that we never are able to settle that truth decisively. But what could possibly be responsible for the truth here? Certainly it is not just a matter of our own fantasies or dreams. It is nothing we have made up or invented. It is the fabric, the contours, of mathematical space, or logical space.

Metaphysicians of the deepest sort, such as Plato and Spinoza and Leibniz, also sought to map the truths of logical space. But instead of concerning themselves merely with numbers, sets and shapes, they concerned themselves with our deepest and most powerful concepts, such as *substance, cause, property* and *relation*. They believed there are necessary truths about these concepts as well, such as that every substance has a cause, and that substances are more basic ("more real") than the relations they bear to one another. The broader context into which Spinoza projects his god is the austere space of *metaphysical necessity*, which is just as rarefied and pure as the Euclidean space that forces upon us the truth that the sum of a triangle's angles is equal to two right angles.

The change in backdrop, as we shall see, makes all the difference in the world. The traditional Judaeo-Christian metaphysical backdrop, whatever its details, allows for the existence of a divine person who has features somewhat familiar to ours (even if theologians understand those features to be only "analogical" to ours). God has a plan, invests the world with a purpose, pronounces judgements, acts with love, mercy and justice, and so on. All this goes far beyond anything reason can teach. So it takes more than reason to enter into a relationship with this divine person; it takes *faith*, or "the assurance of things hoped for, the conviction of things not seen" (Heb. 11:1). But Spinoza's God requires no such faith, as the one substance is fully fathomable by reason. We enter into "a relationship" with it precisely through our employment of reason, the very same organ allowing us to perform geometrical constructions and produce deductive arguments, as well as recognize the truth of axioms. Rational insight and cogitation is, for Spinoza, the analogue of entering into a meditative state or an episode of divine bliss: for it is in such endeavours that we join our minds with the very same metaphysical space that allows for – no, *strictly requires*, if Spinoza is right – the existence of the one substance.

THE ARGUMENT FOR THE ONE SUBSTANCE:
THE THREE KEY IDEAS

Establishing the existence of God, for Spinoza, is like a mathematician establishing the existence of a set that is bigger than the set of natural numbers. One starts with definitions and self-evident axioms and then begins to establish a series of lesser conclusions leading up to the final one. It is like building a bridge into the air: we start with what is on hand, and what seems conceptually sound, and then we carefully combine our elements into structures that carry us out into the beyond. The elements Spinoza makes use of from the start are foundational metaphysical terms, such as substance, essence and attribute. His strategy is to show that the proper understanding of these terms carries us to a conclusion that reaches well beyond our ordinary experience. It is, therefore, important to focus as tightly as possible on the terms without trying to match them to elements of our ordinary experience.

The simplest way to approach Spinoza's argument, and thus to gain a deeper appreciation of the nature of Spinozistic theology, is to establish three key ideas he uses to reach his conclusion that there is and can be only one substance.

I. A substance is, by its nature, a world apart from everything else

Many notions of substance have been offered through the history of philosophy. But at the core of each theory is the idea that a substance is, in one way or another, *self-sufficient* in its existence. Substances are supposed to be the key players in the universe. Typically (although with some notable exceptions) they are taken to be the things that are created and born, undergo changes and cause effects, interact with one another, and eventually die or decay. They may have some degree of dependence on one another for their existence: humans, for example, are indebted to their mothers and fathers for bringing them into existence. And theists generally believe that absolutely all created substances depend on God to preserve them in existence at each moment. So substances do not stand entirely alone. Still, substances are thought to

34

have *greater ontological self-sufficiency* than other sorts of things, such as any properties they may have or relations they may have with one another. Another way of making this point is to say, with Aristotle, that substances are the subjects of predication. This is not merely the claim that the names of substances usually occupy the "subject" part of a complete grammatical sentence. It is rather to say that when we talk about the world, we talk first and foremost about what happens to substances. Talk of properties and relations is somehow derivative of our talk of substances. They are the "players" in the universe.

As I said, most philosophers do not insist that substances are *wholly* self-sufficient. If they did, then hardly anything would rank as a substance. All the familiar things around us, and we ourselves, would not count as substances, since none of us bring ourselves into being, and no one could exist for long in a total vacuum. If we were to insist that in order to be a substance a thing had to be *totally* self-sufficient, then the only things that would rank as substances would be necessary beings or *gods*: entirely self-sufficient beings with no need of anything external to themselves. Descartes adopted this strong view and claimed that, strictly speaking, God is the only true substance (*Principles of Philosophy* 1.51; Descartes [1619–50] 1985: I, 210). But then he hastened to introduce the notion of a *created substance*, or that which needs only the concurrence of God to exist. A created substance is in effect a middle-class substance, one that is more self-sufficient than a quality or property is, but not as self-sufficient as a necessary being or a god.

Spinoza prefers to speak strictly. His focus is on the *concept* of substance, not on how that concept might be applied to the objects of our sense experience. And the core concept of a substance is the concept of a self-sufficient being, both ontologically and conceptually: "By substance I understand what is in itself and is conceived through itself, i.e., that whose concept does not require the concept of another thing, from which it must be formed" (*Ethics* ID3). This definition has two parts. The first is ontological: a substance is *in* itself, meaning that it needs no other thing to bring it into existence or sustain it in existence. The second is conceptual: a substance is *conceived through itself*, meaning that it does not imply the existence of anything other than itself. There is a sense that, according to Spinoza, a substance must stand absolutely independently of everything else, ontologically and conceptually. Each substance is a world unto itself, so to speak, utterly divorced in every possible way from any other possible substance. This, Spinoza thinks, is the very root of the concept of *substance*: ontological self-sufficiency than which none greater can be conceived.

II. It is senseless to distinguish two substances that are essentially the same

Put that way, it sounds rather obvious, but in fact this key idea is one of Spinoza's most radical metaphysical claims. In the *Ethics* it is stated as follows: "In nature there cannot be two or more substances of the same nature or attribute" (*Ethics* IP5). A nature or attribute is the *essence* of a substance, or a final answer to the question "What *kind* of thing is that substance?" Descartes believed that each substance in nature was one or the other of two basic kinds: the extended, bodily kind and the thinking kind. There are the things that take up space and there are the entities that are somehow able to *represent* things, to think of their ideas and concepts. Nowhere in the physical world will we find the mental representation of a triangle; at the very most we may be able to locate some region of the brain that "lights up" when a person thinks about triangles, but nowhere in that lit-up region will a triangle be found. The "thought-of" triangle exists in a different space, somehow, a representational or intentional space, a space touched only by thought and unmeasured by metre sticks; and that sort of existence seemed to Descartes (as it still seems to many) to be a different kind of thing altogether from existing in physical space. Thus Cartesian dualism: there is the world of bodies and the world of thoughts, and the two are utterly distinct.

Descartes never doubted whether two different individuals could be essentially the same. Two bodies are distinct individuals, but are the same kind of thing, namely, the spatial or extended kind. Two ideas or two minds are distinct from one another but are essentially the same kind of thing. But in thinking about bodies and minds Descartes was not thinking of true, full-blown, Spinozistic substances, the radically self-contained things that are worlds apart from one another. If we insist on thinking about such true substances, then it is impossible that there are two substances that are essentially the same. What would make them distinct from one another? What would tell us we were conceiving two identical twins, as opposed to the same individual twice over?

Spinoza provides a brief demonstration for the claim that substances cannot share attributes at *Ethics* IP5, but he provides a fuller defence in an earlier work, his *Principles of Cartesian Philosophy*. Spinoza is defending Descartes' claim that there cannot be more than one god; but clearly his line of argument could also be used to show that there cannot be two substances that share an essence:

> Conceive, if possible, that there is more than one god, e.g., A and B. Then both A and B must, in the highest degree, understand, i.e., A understands everything, including both himself and B, and B, in turn, will understand himself and A. But since A and B exist necessarily, then the cause of the truth and necessity of the idea of B which is in A, is B. Conversely, the cause of the truth and necessity of the idea of A which is in B is A. Consequently, there will be a perfection in A which is not from A, and one in B which is not from B. So neither A nor B will be gods.
>
> (pt I, prop. 11, demo.; Curley, 254–5)

The main idea is that if there were two gods, A and B, then the idea of god A, which is included in the understanding of god B, would be true in virtue of god A, and vice versa. This would ultimately contradict the self-contained nature of a god: any god who relied on another god for the ground of the truth of his ideas would not be an ultimately perfect, self-contained being (as any god ought to be). Thus the general lesson would be that rich accounts of "world-apart" entities, like substances, cannot make necessary reference to other entities without undermining the world apartness of those entities.

III. The bare possibility of a substance is sufficient for its existence (provided, that is, no other better-founded substance gets in its way)

We saw, in connection with the second key idea, that substances have natures or essences. A substance's nature or essence is defined by Spinoza as an attribute, or "what the intellect perceives of a substance, as constituting its essence" (*Ethics* ID4). Descartes thought each substance (or created substance) had exactly one essence, or "principal" attribute, which could be either extendedness or thinkingness. Attributes, like substances, are worlds apart from one another. The ultimate natures or essences do not rely on any other essence or nature for their existence or their intelligibility. The nature of extendedness does not force us to infer anything about the existence of thinkingness or its nature; and the same goes for the nature of thinkingness.

Given the separateness of attributes, it is a little puzzling why Descartes thought each thing could have only one essence. If essence A and essence B have absolutely nothing to do with one another, what possible contradiction could result from claiming that some substance is essentially both A and B? Perhaps Descartes' line of thought was that if A and B are so totally "world apart" from one another, then no single thing could harbour them both. And, indeed, it is difficult to see how an essentially extended thing, as Descartes understands it, could be capable of thought, or how an entity in the world of thought (the triangle we conceive, for instance) could be measured by an actual measuring stick.

But Spinoza never fears to follow where the arguments lead him, and in this case the argument is one that Leibniz displayed to him one day when they met in the Hague in 1676. Leibniz thought Spinoza's argument for God's existence was incomplete, since he thought that it must first be shown that God, as Spinoza defines God, is genuinely possible. So Leibniz provided his own demonstration that all attributes (or "perfections") are indeed compossible, in other words, that one substance can have them all:

> By a *perfection* I mean every simple quality which is positive and absolute or which expresses whatever it expresses without any limits.

But because a quality of this kind is simple, it is unana-lyzable or indefinable, for otherwise it will not be a simple quality but an aggregate of many or, if it is one [among several of the same kind], it will be contained within limits and hence will be understood through a negation of what is beyond these limits; which is contrary to the hypothesis, since it is assumed to be purely positive.

From this it is not difficult to show that *all perfections are compatible with each other* or can be in the same subject.

For let us assume that there is a proposition of this kind: *A and B are incompatible*, understanding by *A* and *B* two simple forms or perfections of this kind … It is clear that this proposition cannot be demonstrated with-out an analysis of the terms *A* and *B*, either or both, for otherwise their nature would not enter into the reason-ing, and incompatibility could be demonstrated equally as well about any other things as about themselves. And by hypothesis they are unanalyzable. Therefore this proposi-tion cannot be demonstrated about them.

(Leibniz/Loemker, 167–8)

Since the proposition that two perfections are incompatible cannot be demonstrated to be true, Leibniz infers that it cannot be necessarily true (since, if it were, it would be demonstrable). Therefore, it is possible for there to be a being with all perfections. Leibniz notes, perhaps with some pride, that Spinoza thought this demonstration is sound at least after Leibniz took the trouble to put it into writing and show it to him.

The reason for going into these considerations about the com-possibility ("being possible together") of attributes is that, for Spinoza, as with any geometer, showing the intelligibility of a conceptual entity is sufficient for showing its existence. In logical space, to be is to be conceivable. And so Spinoza's argument for the existence of substances is about as quick as can be: "A substance cannot be produced by anything else; therefore it will be cause of itself, i.e., its essence necessarily involves existence, *or* it pertains to its nature to exist" (*Ethics* IP7D). Thus if it is possible, it is real.

But there is more to be said than this. For as we ascribe essences or attributes to a substance, predicating extendedness of it, and thinkingness of it and so on, we ascribe reality or being to the substance; the more we say of it, the more it is. Or, as Spinoza claims is "evident" from the definition of attribute, "the more reality or being each thing has, the more attributes belong to it" (*Ethics* IP9).

We shall examine this puzzling claim in more detail in the next section. For now, assume it is true that substances with more attributes are somehow "more real," or have some greater claim to reality. This assumption, if granted, ultimately entails that there can be only one substance: God, or the substance consisting of all possible essences. Here is the argument: (1) Every substance by its very nature exists, and (let us suppose) every substance has at least one essence. But, as we have seen, (2) it is senseless to distinguish substances that are essentially the same: in other words, no essence is shared by two or more substances. Now, if (3) one substance has infinite attributes (that is, if there is no essence the substance lacks), and if substances cannot share attributes (as 2 says), then (Conclusion) there can be no substances other than this one. Thus God is the only substance, q.e.d.

Here we see the relevance of the bracketed qualification in the section heading: that mere possibility is enough to guarantee the existence of a possible substance, *provided no "better-founded" substance gets in the way*. God "gets in the way" of every other possible substance by already expressing every possible attribute. There is nothing more to be expressed, nothing more to be said. God exists in every possible way there is to exist. And God is so good at it, so infinitely thorough at every way of being, that there is no opening for the existence of anything else.

A CLOSER EXAMINATION: WHY ARE SUBSTANCES WITH MORE ATTRIBUTES "MORE REAL"?

We have reached the principal feature of Spinoza's metaphysics: namely, the claim that God is the only substance. And, as we have seen, Spinoza's argument for this conclusion depends crucially on the claim that a substance with more attributes, or more essences, is somehow "better-founded" than a substance with fewer attributes. Because it is so important, we should examine this claim and Spinoza's understanding of it more closely.

As we have seen, Spinoza's basic argumentative strategy is to show that God, as a substance, must exist; and then to show that the existence of God, as a substance with all possible attributes, somehow *rules out* the existence of any other possible substance. But let us pause to consider: why should God rule out the existence of other possible substances, instead of the other way round? Why can't some other lowly substance somehow win the race and then preclude God from coming into existence?[1] Consider, in this vein, an alternative version of Spinoza's argument that instead favours one of God's rivals – Monos, a substance with just one attribute:

1. It pertains to the nature of a substance to exist.
2. Therefore, it pertains to the nature of Monos (a being defined as having just one attribute) to exist.
3. But no two substances (being "a world apart") can share the same attribute.
4. Therefore, God cannot exist.

Why should God prevail over Monos? While Spinoza does not consider this objection explicitly, his response to it would be that substances with more attributes have a greater *propensity* to exist than substances with fewer attributes. Let us see what sense can be made of this claim.

In support of this "propensity" claim, we must turn specifically to *Ethics* IP9, a proposition that is something of an idle wheel in Spinoza's geometrical machine, since it is supposedly derived from a definition and is never employed explicitly in any later demonstration. It states: "The more reality or being each thing has, the more attributes belong to it". God gets priority, it seems, because even as a possible substance he is somehow more real than any other substance, since God has more attributes. Thus God has some ontological edge over Monos.

But, at least initially, it is hard to see why this proposition should be true. Spinoza demonstrates it by claiming that it is "evident" from his definition of "attribute", which is "what the intellect perceives of a substance, as constituting its essence". But it is not evident: even if an attribute is perceived as an essence, why should it follow that substances with more attributes are *more real* than those with fewer attributes?

We can supply a technical answer on Spinoza's behalf by bestowing upon him a *doctrine of propensities*:

T1. Each possible substance *s* has a propensity *P* to exist. ["*P(s)*"]
T2. Each possible substance *s* has a number of essences *E*. ["*E(s)*"]
T3. For all possible beings *x*, *P(x)* is proportional to *E(x)*.

From this doctrine, and from the definition "attribute", it does indeed follow that substances with more essences have greater propensities to exist. But of course this is just a repair in the logic. It does not reveal what it really means for one possible substance to "gain an ontological edge" over another possible substance in the race to existence.

Spinoza seems to have regarded proposition IP9 and something like the doctrine of propensities as obvious. Early on, in the *Short Treatise*, he wrote: "the more essences one ascribes to [a being], the more attributes one must also ascribe to it. So if a being is infinite, its attributes must also be infinite, and that is precisely what we call a perfect being" (pt I, ch. 2; Curley, 69). And in Letter 9 (written shortly after the publication of the *Short Treatise*), as he explained his definition of "God" to a correspondent, Spinoza wrote:

> [N]othing is more evident to us than that we conceive each being under some attribute, and that the more reality or being a being has the more attributes must be attributed to it; so a being absolutely infinite must be defined, etc.   (*Letters* 9, to De Vries)

He followed this claim with the claim that "the more attributes I attribute to a being the more I am compelled to attribute existence to it".[2] These quotes, taken together, suggest something along the lines of the doctrine of propensities, although, of course, they suggest only that Spinoza believed the doctrine and do not explain how the doctrine could be true.

One possible argument for the thought behind the doctrine of propensities can be found in Descartes. Descartes writes that the more we attribute to a substance, the more reason we have for taking the substance to be real. Perhaps his idea is that each time I affirm that a substance is X, and is Y, and is Z, and so on, I affirm that the substance *is* something, and so affirm the existence of the substance. In considering this line of thought, we should note that Descartes could not mean that I can make a thing "more real" *simply* by making predications of it. There are many ridiculous predications that can be made of the humblest things ("This glob is smelly; it is smelly to you, and smelly to me; it is smelly on the mountain tops, and on the sparkling shores ..."), and there is no reason why these predications should make anything more real. Instead, the predications that are made must be of a more significant nature, such as predicating additional *essences* of a thing. But, still, we may be left wondering why this should be true.

Leibniz also took the doctrine of propensities to be obvious. In a 1697 document entitled "On the First Principles of Creation", Leibniz writes:

> [W]e should first acknowledge that from the fact that something exists rather than nothing, there is a certain urgency [*exigentia*] toward existence in possible things or in possibility or essence itself – a pre-tension to exist, so to speak – and, in a word, that essence in itself tends to exist. From this it follows further that all possible things, or things expressing an essence or possible reality, tend toward existence with equal right in proportion to the quantity of essence or reality, or to the degree of perfection which they involve; for perfection is nothing but quantity of essence. (Leibniz/Loemker, 487)

Leibniz's reasoning here is *a posteriori*: we acknowledge from the fact that there is something rather than nothing that there must be some inclination on the part of possible things to exist. And, furthermore, this inclination is stronger in proportion to the "quantity" or amount of essence. But there is not an explanation for this claim to be found here, and the tone of Leibniz's discussion suggests that he thinks the doctrine is merely a fact to be acknowledged.

In the end, it may be that Spinoza and Leibniz (and their Latin readers) took the doctrine of propensities to be obvious just because of a particular linguistic fact. There is an obvious etymological similarity between the Latin word for essence (*essentia*) and the Latin verb "to exist" (*esse*). Once one assumes that it makes sense to think of possible beings as having varying degrees of reality or being, then it may seem linguistically obvious that the more *essentiae* a thing has, the more *esse* it has. John F. Wippel, in explaining Ockham's identification of essence with existence, notes that

> the Latin term "*esse*" can be taken either as a noun or as a verb. When it is used in the first way ["being"], it signifies the same thing as essence and even in the same grammatical and logical mode. When taken in the second way ["to be"], "*esse*" signifies a verb that which "essence" signifies as a noun. (Wippel 1982: 402)

So Spinoza may have thought it was obvious that the number of essences correlates with the degree of being, in exactly the same way that it might seem obvious that the quantity of one's *riches* correlates with how *rich* one is.

But in any event, if Spinoza did think it was obvious, not everyone agreed. The addressee of Letter 9, Simon de Vries, did not think it was obvious even that a substance could have more than one attribute, let alone that one of them with many attributes had a greater propensity to exist. At this point, it is not clear what further defence can be made for the claim that substances with more essences are ontologically better-founded.

A CLOSER EXAMINATION: ATTRIBUTES

We should take a moment to clarify the relation between substances and attributes, particularly in the case where a substance has many attributes. Spinoza defines God as "a substance *consisting* [*constantem*, from *constare*] of an infinity of attributes" (*Ethics* ID6, emphasis added). "To consist of" is one way to translate "*constare*" (and both Curley and Shirley do so), but it is not the only way; in classical sources it far more frequently means *to be in agreement with* or *to cohere with*. But in any case, the definition has caused commentators to wonder how a substance can consist of, agree with or cohere with an *infinity* of attributes. Does this make the one substance infinitely complex? That cannot be, as Spinoza thinks of God as being utterly indivisible (*Ethics* IP11, IP12). Is it to ascribe infinitely many properties of God? That may sound unexceptionable, but are we to understand the one substance to be anything itself *apart from* all those attributes or properties?

Some light can be shed on this definition by considering the *constituent ontology* favoured by many scholastic philosophers.[3] According to a constituent ontology, a substance is not properly said to "have" a nature (or essence or attribute); it instead *is* that nature. Adam, for example, *is* human. This is not to say that Adam *has* the property of being human; for what would that Adam who has that property be? Instead, each substance is *what-it-is-as-such*; in Adam's case, Adam is human-as-such. The same is true of Eve. Now, according to the scholastics, finite entities like Adam and Eve are not *merely* humans-as-such. Adam's matter is distinct from Eve's matter, their forms differ slightly, Adam has lived a little longer, and so on. But as far as their natures are concerned, they are one and the same. And, again, this is not to say they share a property. Rather, it is to say that the same nature – in this case, *humanity* – composes each of them. The best way to state the matter is the straightforward one: they *are* human.

So let us apply this to Spinoza's one substance: the attributes of Spinoza's one substance, understood as essences or natures of that substance, are neither thing-like parts of it nor properties of it. Each attribute *is* that substance – God *is* extension, God *is* thought – just as a body *is* extension (in Descartes' philosophy) or Adam *is* human (in the scholastic constituent ontology). This is to say, as Spinoza does, that the one substance *consists* of its attributes; the attributes *constitute* the one substance's essence. The attributes are nothing apart from the substance, and the substance is not anything apart from them.

A CLOSER EXAMINATION: THE RELATION OF
ATTRIBUTES TO THE INTELLECT

Spinoza defines an "attribute" as *what the intellect perceives of a substance as pertaining to* its essence (*Ethics* ID4). Much scholarly ink has been spilled over the role of the intellect in relation to the ontological status of attributes. Does Spinoza mean that attributes are somehow illusory? That they are subjective ways in which we conceive the one substance? Or has he slipped in an epistemological notion where none is needed?

If we turn to Descartes' discussion of the relation between substances and their primary attributes, we can easily see why Spinoza invokes the intellect in his definition of "attribute". Furthermore, understanding this will help us to shore up our understanding of substance's relation to its attributes. Descartes defines a primary attribute as that "which constitutes its nature and essence" (*Principles of Philosophy* 1:53; Descartes [1619–50] 1985: I, 210). But when it comes to distinguishing substances from their attributes, the distinction is at most a *conceptual distinction*. As Descartes explains:

> a *conceptual distinction* is a distinction between a substance and some attribute of that substance without which the substance is unintelligible; alternatively, it is a distinction between two such attributes of a single substance. Such a distinction is recognized by our inability to form a clear and distinct idea of the substance if we exclude from it the attribute in question, or, alternatively, by our inability to perceive clearly the idea of one of the two attributes if we separate it from the other. (*Principles of Philosophy* 1:62; Descartes [1619–50] 1985: I, 214)

Descartes' point is that we can separate in thought a substance and its attribute, or two attributes, even though it is naturally impossible for that substance to exist without that attribute, or perhaps even for those attributes to exist in separate substances. This means that an extended substance is only conceptually distinct from its extension, and that a thinking substance is only conceptually distinct from its thought. Indeed, Descartes makes this point explicitly in the next article:

> Thought and extension can be regarded as constituting the natures of intelligent substance and corporeal substance; they must then be considered as nothing else but thinking substance itself and extended substance itself – that is, as mind and body. In this way we will have a very clear and distinct understanding of them. Indeed, it is much easier for us to have an understanding of extended substance or thinking substance than it is for us to understand substance on its own, leaving out the fact that it thinks or is extended. For we have some difficulty in abstracting the notion of substance from the notions of thought and extension, since the distinction between these notions and the notion of substance itself is merely a conceptual distinction. (*Principles of Philosophy* 1:63; Descartes [1619–50] 1985: I, 215)

When Descartes claims that thought and extension "must then be considered as nothing else but thinking substance itself and extended substance itself", he means to claim that the first substance *just is* thought and the second substance *just is* extension; the distinction between the substances and their attributes is, again, merely a conceptual one. Of course, more of a story needs to be told in order to show how two bodies are to be distinguished from one another, if each *just is* extension. The outline of Descartes' story should be familiar: substance 1 is *this* bit of extension, with *this* shape and *this* motion, while substance 2 is *that* bit of extension, with *that* shape and *that* motion. The bodies are distinguished by their modes. But these are accidental differences; there is nothing more to the *nature* or *essence* of each substance than extension.

Now we can apply this view to Spinoza, at least to clear up why the intellect is mentioned in his definition of "attribute": Spinoza, in claiming that an attribute is what the intellect perceives of a substance, as constituting its essence, is only claiming that the distinction between a substance and its attributes is merely conceptual. A substance *just is* its attributes, although we can distinguish them in thought. A substance cannot really exist without them, and they cannot really exist without the substance, and – since as a matter of fact there is only one substance with all the attributes – the attributes cannot really exist without one another. Thus the only distinction to be made between a substance and its attributes or among attributes is a distinction to be made by an intellect. Spinoza indeed could have defined "attribute" just as the essence of a substance, but that raises the question of what sort of distinction there is between a substance and its essence. By adding "what the intellect perceives", Spinoza indicates that the difference is conceptual.

Of course, this opens the path to the following inference: if extension *is* God, and thought *is* God, then it follows transitively that extension *is* thought – which seems absurd. But if this interpretation is correct, Spinoza would not regard this consequence as absurd, at least not if it were stated with a little more care: that is to say, the distinction between extension and thought is *merely conceptual*. Consider what he says at *Ethics* IIP7S: "the thinking substance and the extended substance are one and the same substance, which is now comprehended under this attribute, now under that". Extension *is* thought, although we do distinguish them conceptually.

Although he can identify the attributes in a sense, Spinoza does need to insist that there is a stark conceptual barrier between thought and extension since, when it comes to providing explanations, he certainly does not allow any mixing:

> Hence, so long as things are considered as modes of thinking, we must explain the order of the whole of nature, or the connection of causes, through the attribute of Thought alone. And insofar as they are considered as modes of Extension, the order of the whole of nature must be explained through the attribute of Extension alone. I understand the same concerning the other attributes.
>
> (*Ethics* IIP7S)

Each attribute is merely conceptually distinct from the one substance. But each attribute is its own world, in a sense: each is completely self-contained conceptually. Spinoza would certainly deny that clearly and distinctly understanding one attribute would require understanding any other attribute: each can stand totally alone. This radical conceptual independence would, at first, seem to make the attributes *really* distinct from the others, since Descartes claims in *Principles of Philosophy* 1:60 that substances are really distinct when one can be conceived without the others. But also recall the passage quoted above, from *Principles of Philosophy* 1:62, where Descartes writes, "a *conceptual distinction* is a distinction between a substance and some attribute of that substance without which the substance is unintelligible; *alternatively, it is a distinction between two such attributes of a single substance*" (Descartes [1619–50] 1985: I, 214, emphasis added).

The second claim voices a second, alternative definition of "conceptual distinction": it obtains between two attributes that are each merely conceptually distinct from a single substance. There is no mention made of whether those two attributes can be conceived without one another. One might suspect that these two attributes will always involve one another indirectly, since they are attributes of the same substance. But in the Cartesian framework this is not necessarily so. Consider a body with duration and extension. It is true that if we consider extension, we will then necessarily consider a body (a vacuum is impossible in Cartesian philosophy); and if we consider a body, we will necessarily consider it existing over some duration. But suppose we begin instead by considering duration. We may then go on to consider either a body or a mind, and in only the former case will we necessarily consider extension. So it follows that there can be attributes that are merely conceptually distinct from one another, where one can be conceived adequately without the other. In Descartes' metaphysics, though, it seems that this is only possible in the case where we have a principal and a non-principal attribute, and we begin by considering the non-principal one.

If by "attribute" we mean only "principal attribute", and if it were possible for a substance to have multiple principal attributes – and these conditions apply to Spinoza's metaphysics – then every attribute would indirectly involve all the others. For each attribute would lead us necessarily to consider the one substance, whose essences are all the attributes. But, as we shall see, it is important that this involvement among the attributes remain indirect. For Spinoza enforces a conceptual barrier among the attributes, such that no explanation of phenomena of one attribute will appeal to phenomena of another attribute. Of course, there must always be an indirect, metaphysical connection: any phenomenon of any attribute will be phenomena of the one substance, which consists of all possible attributes.

Now a constituent ontology is well behaved if each substance has only one nature or attribute, as in Descartes' metaphysics. It is also well behaved if each substance has natures that in some sense go together: for example, Adam might have not only a human nature, but a nature as an animate being, as a material being, and so on. Duns Scotus, for one, held each of these "formalities" was "in" Adam. But in the case of Spinoza, the constituent ontology makes his metaphysics seem very strange, although it is strange in the right sort of way, a way that suggests we have interpreted Spinoza correctly. For example, we have already seen that Spinoza must believe that the distinction between a thinking substance and an extended substance is merely conceptual. This is directly opposed to Cartesian intuitions, which suggest that extension and thought are so radically different from one another that no substance could have both natures.

We can see this point being made in quasi-dramatic form in a strange little dialogue Spinoza offers in his *Short Treatise*. Lust, a villainous character, claims that "I see that intellectual substance has nothing to do with extended substance", and heroic Reason responds:

[I]f you want to call the corporeal and the intellectual [both] "substances" in respect to the modes which depend on them, you must equally call them modes too, in relation to the substance on which they depend. In the same way that you call willing, sensing, understanding, loving, etc., different modes of what you call thinking substance ..., so I also infer, by your own proof, that infinite extension and thought, together with other infinite attributes (or as you would say, substances) are nothing but modes of that unique, eternal, infinite Being, existing through itself; and of all these we make (as we have said) One Unique being or Unity, outside which we cannot imagine anything.   (Curley, 75)

Reason thus proposes to make extension and thought, together with other infinite attributes, "modes" of the one substance, or somehow reliant upon it, in just the same way that willing, sensing and loving are considered generally to be modes of a thinking substance. Spinoza is moving between these terms here with a certain degree of sloppiness, but his point is obvious: the apparently vast difference between thought and extension is not reason enough, he thinks, to conclude that they may belong only to really distinct beings.

After all, as Spinoza urges in *Ethics* IP10S, thought and extension are entirely distinct, conceptually; hence, there is no absurdity in claiming that one substance has both of them as attributes:

From these propositions it is evident that although two attributes may be conceived to be really distinct (i.e., one may be conceived without the aid of the other), we still cannot infer from that that they constitute two beings, or two different substances. For it is of the nature of a substance that each of its attributes is conceived through itself, since all the attributes it has have always been in it together, and one could not be produced by another, but each expresses the reality, or being of substance.

So it is far from absurd to attribute many attributes to one substance. Indeed, nothing in nature is clearer than that each being must be conceived under some attribute, and the more reality, or being it has, the more it has attributes which express necessity, or eternity, and infinity. And consequently there is also nothing clearer than that a being absolutely infinite must be defined (as we taught in ID6) as a being that consists of infinite attributes, each of which expresses a certain eternal and infinite essence.

Since Spinoza makes the effort to explain why it is "far from" absurd to attribute many attributes to one substance, we may suppose that he expected at least some of his readers to think it *is* absurd. The absurdity is not hard to locate: how can one thing have both thinking and extended natures? Admittedly, there seems to be no contradiction in assuming that a thing does; and most Christians, at any rate, are used to attributing various natures to God – or at least thinking of God as both three really distinct persons and a substance of a single essence.[4] In a later passage, Spinoza even makes a rare attempt to use scripture in support of his conception of God: in *Ethics* IIP7S, as he tries to explain how a mode of extension and the idea of that mode are one and the same thing, conceived under different attributes, he claims that "some of the Hebrews seem to have seen this, as if through a cloud, when they maintained that God, God's intellect, and the things understood by him are one and the same". Furthermore, as we have seen, Descartes, in explaining what a "conceptual distinction" means in *Principles of Philosophy* 1:62, writes of a single substance having multiple attributes, each of which is only conceptually distinct from the substance itself. This draws his position closer to admitting the possibility of attributing more than one principal attribute to a single substance.

WHAT COULD THIS POSSIBLY MEAN?

In this concluding section we shall pull back to a more general level. We have seen the strategy of Spinoza's "geometrical demonstration" of substance monism, or the claim that there can exist only one substance. But as with most *a priori* demonstrations, it is initially hard to see the significance of what has been shown. What does his saying that there is only one substance really amount to?

First and foremost, it is to claim that *everything is one*. Spinoza's metaphysics asserts there to be a profound unity in nature. This assertion contradicts the conclusion generally suggested by experience. We see diversity in things, not unity. We see planets and anthills, economic downturns and slabs of concrete. And sometimes, as we plumb our experience in deeper and more philosophical ways, we see only fragments that seemingly can never be assembled into a whole. How can Spinoza bridge his intellectual assurance that all is one with the testimony of human experience that real things are ultimately very different from each other?

We shall pursue this question in greater detail in Chapter 4, but for now we may look again to Spinoza's dialogue between Lust and Reason, this time with the broader question of how to find unity in disunity. Spinoza takes up the apparently deep divide in Cartesian philosophy between the abstract world of ideas and the thumping world of concrete bodies. Lust, for his (her?) part, is confident that there is no unity in nature; for Lust lives by appearances, and appearances suggest pluralism, and perhaps even chaos.

> LUST: I see that intellectual substance has nothing to do with extended substance ... and if, in addition to these substances, you want to posit still a third, which is perfect in everything, then you will involve yourself in manifest contradictions. For if this third substance is posited, apart from the other two, it will lack all the attributes which pertain to these two. And this is impossible in a [unified] whole, outside which no thing is. (Curley, 74)

In brief, Lust sees that the world of the mind and the world of bodies have nothing in common with one another. And if someone wishes to abstractly define some kind of third, perfect substance that serves to unify them – perhaps an amalgam of "bodymind", like "spacetime" – then it will have to be somehow distinct from each of them in order to be real in its own right. So in the end we shall have even greater diversity, not less. Thus, according to Lust, the absolute irreducibility of mind to body or of body to mind entails the falsity of monism.

But, to present again the passage given above, Reason believes it can see unity where Lust cannot:

> REASON: [I]f you want to call the corporeal and the intellectual [both] substances in respect to the modes which depend on them, you must equally call them modes too, in relation to the substance on which they depend. In the same way that you call willing, sensing, understanding, loving, etc., different modes of what you call thinking

substance ..., so I also infer, by your own proof, that infinite extension and thought, together with other infinite attributes (or, as you would say, substances) are nothing but modes of that unique, eternal, infinite Being, existing through itself; and of all these we make (as we have said) One Unique being or Unity, outside which we cannot imagine anything. (Curley, 75)

In this passage Reason tries to turn Lust's argument against itself. Lust thinks it is obvious that bodies and minds are distinct substances that have absolutely nothing in common. But, Reason suggests, bodies and minds can each have modes (or properties) that are different from one another: the selfsame Socrates can sit and talk, and the selfsame Plato can love and think. So what is to stop us from taking bodies and minds themselves to be different modes of a single substance? Reason sees this as the way to preserve unity in nature despite the apparent diversity, and it is obvious to Reason that there must be such unity.

Spinoza's metaphysical monism also allows for a profound unity in knowledge. Perhaps the finest expression of this unity is found in an unfinished work of Spinoza's, the *Treatise on the Emendation of the Intellect*:

As for order, to unite and order all our perceptions it is required and reason demands that we ask as soon as possible whether there is a certain being, and at the same time what sort of being it is, which is the cause of all things, so that its objective essence may also be the cause of all our ideas and then our mind will (as we have said) reproduce Nature as much as possible. For it will have Nature's essence, order, and unity objectively. (Curley, 41)

Of course, Spinoza thinks there is such a being. Moreover, he thinks the human mind does have an adequate idea of God, so we have within ourselves the objective essence – that is to say, the *content* – of Nature's order and unity. What this means is that our own reason has within itself sufficient resources for constructing a fully adequate model of reality's deepest abiding features, so we have within ourselves the resources for gaining a general understanding of the whole of nature.

But the unity Spinoza tries to establish in the universe and in our knowledge has a special cost. Spinoza's single substance, precisely because of its role as a grand unifier, cannot possibly have some of the qualities people long for in a divine person. The function it performs is perfectly general and universal, with no partiality or particularity. It must, therefore, lack any qualities that allow us to connect to it as persons. Our intellects may well be satisfied but that is not the only, or even primary, goal of a theology.

This cost was brought out in sharp relief by an interaction between Albert Einstein and the theologian Paul Tillich at a conference on science, philosophy and religion in 1940. At the conference, Einstein criticized traditional religious views as being rooted in childish and superstitious anthropomorphism and championed in its place a thoroughly rationalistic kind of reverence toward the unity found in nature:

> It is in this striving after the rational unification of the manifold that [science] encounters its greatest successes, even though it is precisely this attempt which causes it to run the greatest risk of falling a prey to illusions. But whoever has undergone the intense experience of successful advances made in this domain, is moved by profound reverence for the rationality made manifest in existence. By way of the understanding he achieves a far-reaching emancipation from the shackles of personal hopes and desires, and thereby attains that humble attitude of mind toward the grandeur of reason incarnate in existence, and which, in its profoundest depths, is inaccessible to man. This attitude, however, appears to me to be religious, in the highest sense of the word. And so it seems to me that science not only purifies the religious impulse of the dross of its anthropomorphism but also contributes to a religious spiritualization of our understanding of life.   (Einstein 1954: 49)

"The grandeur of reason incarnate in existence": this is perhaps the most poetical characterization of Spinoza's substance monism ever made. Both Spinoza and Einstein saw the cosmos as infused with a profoundly impersonal reason, a unifying architecture that pulls every seemingly disparate entity into itself and renders it both knowable and absolutely indispensable. Both Einstein and Spinoza believe understanding the profound unity of nature *purifies* the religious impulse, washing away "the dross of its anthropomorphism" and revealing a deeper unity that is truly worthy of intellectual wonder and reverence. The passage from Einstein signals only one difference between the two: Einstein believed that the deepest aspects of unity are inaccessible to human beings, while Spinoza puts nothing beyond our grasp.

In his response to Einstein, Tillich argued that this "reason incarnate in existence", so thoroughly impersonal, could not possibly complete the work we require of religion:

> [S]uch a neutral sub-personal cannot grasp the center of our personality; it can satisfy our aesthetic feeling or our intellectual needs, but it cannot convert our will, it cannot overcome our loneliness, anxiety, and despair. For as the philosopher Schelling says: "Only a person can heal a person." This is the reason that the symbol of the Personal God is indispensable for living religion. It is a symbol, not an object, and it never should be interpreted as an object. And it is one symbol besides others indicating that our personal center is grasped by the manifestation of the unaccessible ground and abyss of being.
>
> (Tillich 1959: 132)

Reason can satisfy our intellect, and please our longing for elegant harmonies, but that is not all a human being requires; consider "our loneliness, anxiety, and despair". If we recall, as stated earlier, that the ancient religions project their creators' deepest needs into a metaphysical backdrop, then we may see that there is a need for having a god that is familiar to us: we need healing, and it takes a person to heal a person.

Now Spinoza might well agree that many of us should not abandon these comforting projections. The rest of us (he might say) believe we are ready to face life without them and will let reason, so far as it is able, lead us to a new and revolutionary kind of healing. But more about that in Chapter 4, when we come to Spinoza's psychotherapy of the emotions.

3

The genesis of all things

I think I have shown clearly enough that from God's supreme power, or infinite nature, infinitely many things in infinitely many modes, i.e., all things, have necessarily flowed, or always follow, by the same necessity and in the same way as from the nature of a triangle it follows, from eternity and to eternity, that its three angles are equal to two right angles.   (*Ethics* IP17S)

GEOMETRICAL NECESSITY

Substance monism amounts to the claim that the teeming population of seemingly discrete, finite, changing things is in fact embedded in some unified, infinite, unchanging substance. One further feature of this embedding is also supposed to be perfectly clear, according to Spinoza: the changing things are wholly necessitated by the very nature of the unchanging substance.

Any alternative is unthinkable. Any hint of slippage between the fixtures of the one substance and the existence of finite particulars would constitute a breach of the supreme principle of Spinoza's method for metaphysics, the principle of sufficient reason.[1] If the totality of finite particulars were one set rather than another, or if the totality were one way rather than another, there would have to be some explanation for that fact, and (given the nature of Spinoza's God) the explanation could not be in terms of God's preferences, or in terms of blind chance. God has no preferences, and there is no chance. Just as the structure of logical space requires there to be exactly one substance, the structure of that one substance requires that there be precisely one actual totality of finite particulars – and no other. As Spinoza himself says (with an exaggerated claim to clarity!), "I have shown more clearly than the noon light that there is absolutely nothing in things on account of which they can be called contingent" (*Ethics* IP33S1). What is more, as this chapter's prefatory quote has it, the necessity Spinoza has in mind is the strongest brand of necessity known to him: "From God's nature all things have necessarily flowed by the same necessity as from the nature of a triangle it follows that its three angles are equal to two right angles" (*Ethics* IP17S). Thus do all things issue from God with stark raving *geometrical* necessity.

The task of this chapter is to try to see how God's nature necessitates all things, and in doing so gain a better understanding of the relation between finite things and Spinoza's God. This will also provide the general framework for understanding the nature of finite things in Spinoza's metaphysics, and the sort of life he thinks humans should live, which are the subjects of the following two chapters. What we shall find is that, while Spinoza clearly wants the conclusion that all things are necessitated by the nature of God, there is no single, obvious account within his metaphysics of exactly how this conclusion follows. Still, what is more interesting is the question why Spinoza should want this conclusion at all, since thinkers generally shun necessitarianism (indeed, it was precisely this feature of Spinoza's metaphysics that drove Leibniz away from it). As we shall see, it was Spinoza's *reverence* for the one substance, as he understood it, that brought him to necessitarianism. In his view, a god that does not necessitate the particulars of creation would be a god modelled on human limitations, and that is no god at all.

WHAT FOLLOWS FROM GOD

In the previous chapter we saw that, in some way or other, Spinoza conceived the doctrine of substance monism as a necessary truth. The contours of conceptual necessity demand that there be only one substance consisting of infinite attributes. This one substance and its attributes are called by Spinoza "*natura naturans*" meaning "nature-making nature", or the productive core of existence, God's own active nature, which exists in itself and is conceived through itself (*Ethics* IP29S). He employs this term in order to distinguish God and God's essences from all the things that follow from those essences, the things that rely on God for their existence and for their conceivability. Such dependent things are *natura naturata*, or the "modes" of the one substance.

But it should be noted at the outset that it is not at all obvious why there should be anything other than "nature-making nature" in Spinoza's metaphysics. Spinoza could have followed the Presocratic philosopher Parmenides in claiming that all change is illusory, and in reality there is only one, unchanging thing.[2] In some ways it would have made his metaphysics much smoother sailing. He would face no demand to explain how an eternal and unchanging substance leads to the existence of durational, changing things. His necessitarianism would not have to answer any of the difficulties we shall raise for it later in this chapter. Indeed, it is difficult to see at a general level why Spinoza does not take the Parmenidean path, given the methodological approach his *Ethics* requires. For if we start with only axioms and strict definitions of key concepts, and follow them wherever they lead, then nothing through most of Part I of the *Ethics* should lead us to think that there are any finite individuals at all, just as nothing in Euclid tells us of any particular's actual existence. When finite individuals first are mentioned at *Ethics* IP25C, their appearance seems entirely gratuitous, since it is not implied by any of the previous demonstrations. They arrive on the metaphysical scene as uninvited guests.

But in this case Spinoza is making use of information not provided by his axioms and definitions. He is admitting into his thought what ordinary experience all too plainly teaches, namely, that there are in fact finite, changing things, and our lives are animated by their incessant traffic. The task he then faces as a substance monist is to explain how the finite things of our world follow from the nature of the one substance. The most general answer he provides is that "[f]rom the necessity of the divine nature there must follow infinitely many things in infinitely many modes" (*Ethics* IP16). The one substance's nature is so abundant that a limitless number of things follows from it, including all that we ever experience. But we should try to see more particularly how this "issuing forth" is supposed to happen, and press Spinoza's account with some interpretive difficulties. And we must begin with the technical term Spinoza uses for things other than the one substance.

THE MEANING OF "MODE"

Natura naturata, as we have seen, is the group name for all the products of the active generative power of the one substance. They are what "nature-making nature" *makes.* As Spinoza says, these things following from the one substance are *in* God and are *conceived through* God. When one thing is *in* another through which it is also conceived, Spinoza calls it a "mode" (*Ethics* ID5). To get a fuller sense of the meaning of this term, we need a brief account of the role it played in Spinoza's philosophical context.

Scholastic philosophers prior to Spinoza followed Aristotle in believing that ordinary individuals are substances. Each substance has a set of properties, or what the scholastics called "*real* accidents", which are properties that characterize the substance at a *general* level: the substance is said to be in motion, or shaped, or heated, for example. But no substance has only general properties. The *specific* motion or shape or heat of a substance is understood as a *mode.* So, literally, the mode is the specific *way* (or *modus*) in which the substance is moving, or shaped, or heated. Modes are thus specific determinations of real accidents.

Now the scholastics believed that there is some kind of distinction between a substance and its real accidents. God, for the purpose of illustration, could miraculously sustain real accidents without a subject, or with a change of subject (as in the case of transubstantiation, where the substance of bread is changed into

Christ's body, while still appearing to be bread). Such a distinction between accidents and a substance is not as strong as that which obtains between two separate substances, but it still is a significant one. It is stronger, at any rate, than the distinction between a substance and its modes, since modes are understood ontologically as being *nothing other than* the substance itself in a particular state. Not even God's miraculous power could sustain a *way* of a substance's being without also sustaining the underlying substance itself. Modes cannot march around by themselves. So the particular motion of a body (like moving eastward at a specific speed) *just is* that body moving in that particular way, and similarly for its particular shape or whatever. One of the biggest breaks Descartes made with scholasticism – what he believed would prove to be "the greatest stumbling block" among his readers – was his getting rid of real accidents and treating *all* properties as modes (see Menn 1995).

Spinoza went even further than Descartes. For Descartes, having eliminated real accidents, still inserted something, a buffer, between the modes of a finite body and God, who creates and sustains everything. That buffer is *a body*, a created substance. So, according to Descartes, *God* creates and sustains a *body*, which has a set of *modes*. But Spinoza eliminates the buffer, as he rejects the very notion of a "created substance". So he lets the modes that had belonged to the body belong directly to God. Thus, for Spinoza, everything that is not the one substance itself is a *mode* of the one substance.

Now as Edwin Curley noted long ago, it may seem mistaken at a very basic level to think of particular things as modes, in this sense of the term.[3] For it amounts to conceiving everything in our ordinary experience not as some kind of noun-like thing, but as an adverbial *way* in which the one substance is. This means that you are not a standalone agent, but a *way* in which God is; the moon is not an entity in its own right, but another *way* in which God is; and so on. This may seem queer. But if we follow Descartes in eliminating real accidents, and if we follow Spinoza in his substance monism, this shift in our manner of conceiving finite "things" is a forced move: there simply is nothing else for particulars to be. As the first axiom of the *Ethics* has it, "Whatever is, is either in itself or in another." To be "in itself" is to be a substance, and to be "in another" is to be a mode of a substance. The conclusion that the particulars of experience – and we ourselves – must be in fact mere modes of the one substance is unavoidable in Spinoza's system, although the assertion is both radical and unfamiliar.

INFINITE MODES

Each mode, then, is a way in which the one substance exists. But this does not by itself show why there should be any finite things in Spinoza's metaphysics. Indeed, in one proposition of the *Ethics*, Spinoza seems concerned to ensure that finite modes are kept at an infinite arm's length from God:

> Every singular thing, or anything which is finite and has a determinate existence, can neither exist nor be deter- mined to produce an effect unless it is determined to exist and produce an effect by another cause, which is also finite and has a determinate existence; and again, this cause also can neither exist nor be determined to produce an effect unless it is determined to exist and produce an effect by another, which is also finite and has a determinate exist- ence, and so on, to infinity. (*Ethics* IP28)

In short: to account for the existence of any given finite mode, you always need to suppose another finite mode; and for that another; and so on without end. Spinoza might have employed this argument towards a different conclusion: namely, that from God's infinite nature, no finite thing could ever arise, for such a finite mode would require another, and that another, *ad infinitum*, so there could never be a first finite mode, and so on. But Spinoza does think there *are* finite modes. So why and how should any finite modes arise in the first place?

Spinoza's answer to this question is not clear, but it will have something to do with what he calls "infinite modes". Some modes, although not the finite ones, do issue directly from God and God's attributes. When pressed by a correspondent for examples of these infinite modes, Spinoza offers "in the case of thought, absolutely infinite intellect; in the case of extension, motion and rest" (*Letters* 64, to Schuller). He says a bit more about them in his early work, the *Short Treatise*, where he calls them by another name, the "universal modes" (Curley, 91). These modes "depend on God immediately", and "have been from all eternity, and will remain to all eternity, immutable, a work truly as great as the greatness of the workman". Indeed, in this early work Spinoza calls each infinite mode "a Son" of God, presumably meaning only that they should be seen as God's immediate metaphysical offspring.

Textually, we do not have much more to go on than this. Spinoza's idea seems to be that, given infinite Extension, there follows motion and rest; perhaps what this means is that it is impossible to conceive of any extended region in which movement, or change of place, is not a possibility. Similarly, given Thought, there follows the possibility of every concept that can possibly be formed. Extension is a precondition for movement; Thought is a precondition for every possible idea. There is an ontological asymmetry in that Extension is more fundamental than possible motion, and Thought is more fundamental than any possible idea. But each attribute implies the existence of its infinite mode, and that is what it means to say that the infinite mode follows from the absolute nature of the relevant attribute (*Ethics* IP21).

Now these infinite modes – the possibility of movement, and the possibility of every concept – do not yet yield us any finite things, as these domains each are nothing more than unconstrained possibility. They are each ways, completely comprehensive ways, in which the relevant attribute exists. But there is another infinite mode, following from these two infinite modes, which apparently is meant to deliver the finite things. This third infinite mode follows from the absolute nature of God's attributes, in so far as those attributes are modified by the first two infinite modes. This third infinite mode, that is to say, stands in a "grandson" relation to God. In the same letter mentioned above, Spinoza identifies this third infinite mode with "the face of the whole universe, which, although varying in infinite ways, yet remains always the same", and he refers his correspondent to the *Ethics*, specifically the scholium to lemma 7 preceding IIP14. Let us follow this thread. The scholium to which Spinoza directs us is a discussion of finite bodies joining together to form a more complex body, and such complex bodies joining together to form a body of even greater complexity, which "can be affected in many other ways, without any change in its form". And Spinoza continues: "And if we proceed in this way to infinity, we shall easily conceive that the whole of nature is one Individual, whose parts, i.e., all bodies, vary in infinite ways, without any change of the whole Individual" (*Ethics* IIP13S, lemma 7). This complex individual consisting of all bodies is presumably what Spinoza called "the face of the whole universe", or the infinite mode following from the two immediate infinite modes.

All of this discussion is quite elliptical and murky, but at the very least these texts suggest that the entire universe, comprising all bodies, is an infinite mode of God. Moreover, they suggest that it is an infinite mode that somehow emerges from the possibility of movement in Extension and the possibility of every concept in Thought. In other words – and now perhaps this does not sound wholly implausible – once we have the possibility of movement in space, and the possibility of all ideas, we have all that is needed to conceive a grand totality of bodies and ideas that is the existing universe.[4]

A GUIDING MODEL: DESCARTES'S *WORLD*

In an early work he was reluctant to publish,[5] Descartes asks his readers to imagine a boundless world filled with homogeneous matter. He asks us further to conceive that the matter is "divided into as many parts having as many shapes as we can imagine, and that each of its parts is capable of taking on as many motions as we can conceive" (*The World*, ch. 6; Descartes [1619-50] 1985: I, 91). We further are asked to suppose that God sets all of these parts into motion, in accordance with certain laws of motion that God ensures are followed without exception. Then, claims Descartes, even if we suppose no further directive guidance on God's part, we shall find that:

the laws of nature are sufficient to cause the parts of this chaos to disentangle themselves and arrange themselves in such good order that they will have the form of a quite perfect world – a world in which we shall be able to see not only light but also all the other things, general as well as particular, which appear in the real world.   (*Ibid.*)

This is one expression of the guiding hypothesis of the so-called mechanical philosophy, namely, that matter in a lawfully regulated motion will result in the ordered world we experience.

The rest of *The World* contains Descartes's explanations of how, in this imagined world, all of the phenomena of the actual world would become present (light, sun, stars, planets, comets, tides and so on). It is a *tour de force* of the potential explanatory power of the mechanical philosophy. But one feature Descartes did not advertise is that the overall framework of his thought experiment could also suggest a certain necessitarianism. For we have an infinite sea of matter, set in infinite motion over infinite time. All possible configurations of bodies will eventually turn up, at some place and time or other; every possible arrangement of matter will become actual someplace, sometime. This will include the circumstances in which you and I now find ourselves, as well as countless, *countless* other possibilities. Absolutely anything God could possibly create out of matter in motion will find its way into the actual history of this possible universe, as Descartes has asked us to conceive it. And that is to say that there is nothing possible that is not actual; and another way of making that claim is to say that everything that is actual is necessary.

I am drawing out this feature of Descartes' thought experiment in *The World* because it offers a view of the world that fits neatly with what we have just explained as Spinoza's account of infinite modes. Infinite, homogeneous matter (that is to say, Extension), undergoing all possible movement (an immediate infinite mode) will result in a whole universe of bodies, which undergoes incessant change but maintains a certain lawful constancy in all its changes (the face of the whole universe). If it is indeed true that such circumstances will result in all possible configurations of matter, that is, all possible bodies, then we have as a direct result Spinoza's necessitarianism, or the claim that there is nothing possible that is not actual.[6]

On several occasions Spinoza makes clear that this is exactly the sort of necessitarianism he has in mind: he means to assert that absolutely everything that God (or an infinite intellect) can conceive is made actual at some time or other in the world of bodies. Here are three such occasions (and more can be found easily):

> From the necessity of the divine nature there must follow infinitely many things in infinitely many modes (i.e., everything which can fall under an infinite intellect).
>
> (*Ethics* IP16)

> Therefore, since things could have been produced by God in no other way, and no other order, and since it follows from God's supreme perfection that this is true, no truly sound reason can persuade us to believe that God did not will to create all the things that are in his intellect, with that same perfection with which he understands them.
>
> (*Ethics* IP33S2)

> Whatever we conceive to be in God's power, necessarily exists.
>
> (*Ethics* IP35)

The straightforward sense of such passages is that if anything is possible, it is made actual by God. Nothing that is in any way possible can be kept from existing. There is absolutely nothing in things on account of which they can be called contingent: no entity, not even God, makes a selection from among all possible entities, designating only some of them to become actual. In the jargon of metaphysics, there are no unactualized possibles. This is a necessitarianism than which there could be none stronger.

TWO OBJECTIONS

But there are two reasons for thinking that this straightforward interpretation of Spinoza's necessitarianism is wrong. The first objection is that the view being attributed to Spinoza is (shall we say) *ontologically extravagant*. To get a sense of the extravagance, consider the following thought experiment. Suppose we alter one fact about a finite thing in this world: any fact at all, such as the day on which Spinoza died. Let us make it a day later. Make the necessary changes in *all* the conditions leading to the original fact, and in *all* the consequences issuing from the original fact, in strict accordance with whatever laws of nature issue from the attributes and infinite modes, so that Spinoza ends up dying a day later. The result is a description of a possible state of affairs, and according to the view attributed to Spinoza, this sequence of events *must become actual* at some place and time or other. The result, then, is another planet like Earth, with another Spinoza, its own local past, present and future, existing perhaps in some other distant galaxy or at some other remote time, where the other Spinoza dies a day later. And there is yet another planet like Earth where yet another Spinoza dies a day earlier. *And so on, and on, with every finite fact.*[7] All these other Earths, for every alterable fact, must crop up at some time and place or other in the actual universe. This wild proliferation of planets and galaxies is wild enough to cause us to wonder whether it really could be what Spinoza believed.

On the other hand, we might imagine Spinoza replying that this only shows how extravagantly rich and abundant nature is. And in at least one passage he does in fact say something like this. Toward the very end of part I of the *Ethics*, he considers what should be said in reply to someone who complains about all the imperfections in nature: all the stinking, evil, foolish and revolting features of the world, and especially the human ones. Why should God create such things? Spinoza's answer:

> I answer only "because he did not lack material to create all things, from the highest degree of perfection to the lowest"; or, to speak more properly, "because the laws of his nature have been so ample that they sufficed for producing all things which can be conceived by an infinite intellect" (as I have demonstrated in P16).
>
> (*Ethics*, appendix to part I)

Of course, Spinoza's one substance is impersonal, and it does not have any concern over the virtues or perfections of the modes following from its nature. But Spinoza's answer in this context does not rely on God's lack of personality. It emphasizes instead the broad amplitude of the laws of nature, and the way they allow for the production of all conceivable things, no matter how vicious or imperfect. The strategy of this answer certainly works just as well to answer a complaint about the ontological extravagance of the view under consideration.

The second objection to the straightforward interpretation is that there are places where Spinoza seems to write of things that are possible but never come into existence. The clearest example comes from the appendix to the *Short Treatise*, a work called "Metaphysical Thoughts". Many features in this work are certainly at odds with the views Spinoza later defends in the *Ethics* – it is a work somewhere along the road to mature Spinozism – but one Spinozistic view explicitly espoused by the work is that "a necessity of existing has been in all created things from eternity" (Curley, 309), so in this regard the work does agree with the necessitarian conclusion of the *Ethics*. At any rate, in this work Spinoza writes:

> [I]f we were to conceive the whole of nature, we should discover that many things whose nature we perceive clearly and distinctly, that is, whose essence is necessarily such, can not in any way exist. For we should find the existence of such things in nature to be just as impossible as we now know the passage of a large elephant through the eye of a needle to be, although we perceive the nature of each of them clearly. (Curley, 308)

This indicates that there are some beings that are in some sense *intrinsically* possible (that is, beings "whose nature we perceive clearly and distinctly"), which do not manage to squeeze their way into actuality because their existence somehow is constrained by other restrictive elements in the whole of nature. And Spinoza makes this claim while endorsing necessitarianism. So the straightforward interpretation is evidently not the only way to capture a necessity of existing in all things. It may be true both that all things are necessitated and also that there are some intrinsic possibles that do not make it into actuality.

Moreover, in *Ethics* IIP8 and IIP9, Spinoza writes of "singular things that do not exist" but still reside within God's intellect. But these passages are not quite as clear as the passage from "Metaphysical Thoughts" since the reference might be merely to individuals that do not happen to exist *now*, but have existed or will exist at another time.[8]

These two objections have led at least one prominent interpreter of Spinoza to try to preserve Spinoza's necessitarianism while also allowing that there are modes whose existence would not violate any laws of nature *per se*, but which fail to crop up in the actual sequence of events simply because their causes do not happen to occur.[9] The fundamental idea is that an individual whose full set of causes never crops up in existence is just as impossible, and just as much beyond God's productive power, as an individual whose description is self-contradictory. This would mean, for example, that a child of Héloïse and Abelard, or a seventh Marx brother, or an extra coin in my pocket are all entities that are as impossible as a four-sided triangle or a prime number between three and five. And this will mean claiming that these *seeming* possibles are not conceivable by an infinite intellect, and do not fall within God's productive powers. These, surely, are surprising conclusions but, as we have seen, the fact that a conclusion is surprising is not enough to refrain from attributing it to Spinoza.[10]

But if this is in fact Spinoza's view, then it sits very uncomfortably with a reply he gives to those who believe that God brings into existence less than what is divinely conceivable. Spinoza writes:

> Indeed – to speak openly – my opponents seem to deny God's omnipotence. For they are forced to confess that God understands infinitely many creatable things, which nevertheless he will never be able to create. For otherwise, if he created everything he understood he would (according to them) exhaust his omnipotence and render himself imperfect. Therefore to maintain that God is perfect, they are driven to maintain at the same time that he cannot bring about everything to which his power extends. I do not see what could be feigned which would be more absurd than this or more contrary to God's omnipotence. (*Ethics* IP17S)

71

To be sure, Spinoza's opponent is making a somewhat different claim, something along the lines that if God were to actualize all possibles, he would for some reason exhaust his omnipotence. But Spinoza's reply to this opponent is relevant also to the alternative view we have been considering. For he is saying that anyone who maintains that God "cannot bring about everything to which his power extends" is denying God's omnipotence, and this seems to be exactly what the alternative view we have described is maintaining: specifically, that there are modes or states of affairs that are consistent with the laws of nature (that is, with God's power), but which cannot be brought about (because the relevant causes are lacking). These people, Spinoza is claiming, are placing a limit on God's generative power, and this is something Spinoza judges to be absurd, even with his impersonal conception of God.

At this point we shall pull back from the obscurities in the details of the *how* in Spinoza's necessitarianism, and turn toward the *why*. Why should Spinoza want to claim that everything is necessary?

NECESSITARIANISM AND ESCHATOLOGY

Eschatology is that branch of theology that looks towards what makes things count, in the broadest possible sense. In the end, finally, overall, what matters, and why? There is a sense in which eschatology is theology's very reason for being, inasmuch as religion's chief aim is to tell human beings a story about their own significance – or lack of it. I shall argue that, in affirming necessitarianism, Spinoza eschews any sort of meaningful eschatology.

The other theologies prevalent in Spinoza's day and in our own offer a very different view. Almost all of them allow for some possibility of another world being actual. Some of the more fundamentalist theologies maintain that the overall quality or perfection of our world is in some large part contingent on the prayers we make, the actions we take and the rituals we perform. This view requires that there are several futures available to us. Other more grandiose theologies say, as Leibniz would maintain, that there are infinitely many possible worlds God could create, but God selects the one that is the best in every possible sense. Other theologies might say that it was perfectly possible for the perfect world God did create not to have fallen into depravity and sin, and that our current world is only contingently in that imperfect state. Many theologies will maintain that God has a certain end in mind in creating our world, and the other worlds God might have created would not have attained this end. Certainly any theology that countenances an argument for God's existence based on the beauty, harmony or design present in our world also maintains that the world could have lacked these virtues; for otherwise, the presence of these virtues would not demand any sort of explanation, and this particular argument for God's existence would not even get off the ground.

These non-Spinozistic theologies all agree that *there is some special reason for the way things actually unfold.* It may be that human history is aimed towards a blessed final state, or it may be that the mere presence of free choice and genuine contingency makes this a better world overall than any world lacking these features. This faith that there is a special reason for things being as they are is a basic requirement for *hope.* The hope, in its broadest sense, is that all of the miseries and shortcomings of this world will in some way be turned towards some higher end, and in this way justified. The hope is that there is some vantage point from which it is clear that the way things go is in fact the best way for things to go, all things considered. Out of this hope comes a possibility for *meaning* in our lives. What appears to us as savage, reckless and pointless may in fact be part of a larger plan whose benefit for everyone cannot be doubted.

So denying necessitarianism opens up the possibility of faith, hope and meaningfulness over the broad expanse of human history. This is no small thing; but that is not all. Denying necessitarianism offers hope and meaningfulness in our small-scale decisions as well. As we deliberate over our daily decisions, we cannot help but believe that we have genuine freedom, and that events may go one way, or another. Sometimes the stakes are quite high, and our knowledge is mere guesswork. With the assurance that there is hope and meaningfulness overall, we may have more courage to make the decisions we face, since we have some reason to believe that, in the end, all will come out right. If we lack this assurance, then it will be difficult to resist Sartre's conclusion that human beings are condemned to freedom, making critical decisions with imperfect knowledge and often horrific consequences, which are never balanced out, ever.

It is important to draw out these real benefits of denying necessitarianism in order to see the theological significance of Spinoza's affirming it. In affirming necessitarianism, Spinoza asserts that there is no "special reason" for the actual sequence of events being as it is. Things are as they are simply because there is no other possible way for them to be. Any general hope that the savage and reckless events in our lives will contribute toward a blessed end-state is completely unfounded, and just as misguided and ridiculous as the justifications Pangloss offers Candide. Hope, as Spinoza later defines it, amounts to little more than wishful thinking: "an inconstant Joy, born of the idea of a future or past thing whose outcome we to some extent doubt" (*Ethics* III, Def Aff. XII). If we are to find any meaning in our lives in Spinoza's universe, it will not come from any general assurance that what happens happens for a reason. What happens happens because it must. Hope, faith and meaning are replaced by an affirmation of iron-clad necessity.

Spinoza has nothing but icy disdain for those who believe things can be otherwise. "[A] thing is called contingent only because of a defect of our knowledge", he writes (*Ethics* IP33S1). In a letter, Spinoza drives this point home by asking us to imagine a moving stone that is capable of observing its own motion:

> Now this stone, since it is conscious only of its endeavor and is not at all indifferent, will surely think it is completely free, and that it continues in motion for no other reason than that it so wishes. This, then, is that human freedom which all men boast of possessing, and which consists solely in this, that men are conscious of their desire and unaware of the causes by which they are determined. (*Letters* 58, to Schuller)

Thus we have no such freedom; our belief that we do is as illusory as the stone's would be. All events of the world, including human decisions, are thoroughly necessitated, and not necessitated for any higher end or purpose. Complaining, extolling, praising and blaming are as out of place in human affairs as they would be among pure geometrical solids banging into one another in strict conformity with laws of impact.

If I have succeeded in conveying just how bleak Spinoza's necessitarianism is, then it may come as a surprise to see that his motivation for such a bleak view is a certain species of *reverence* for God. In the lengthy appendix to part I of the *Ethics*, Spinoza provides a kind of genealogy that aims to account for the rise of theologies denying necessitarianism. His account implies that these theologies are rooted in ignorance and confusion, and end up demeaning God through unreasoned anthropomorphism.

Spinoza's genealogy is as follows. First, he claims, humans develop beliefs about what motivates them to act, and how their desires prompt them to manufacture things. We desire shelter from the wind, or food we can farm with some regularity, or winter coats, and generally we are able to produce these things to answer our needs and desires. But then we notice that there are other features in the world, "products", which serve our needs and desires admirably, although neither we nor any other human can take credit for them: for example, "eyes for seeing, teeth for chewing, plants and animals for food, the sun for light, the sea for supporting fish" (*Ethics* I, appendix). We feel we must credit *someone* with these boons, some *powerful* someone, and we assume that this special someone has a psychology similar to our own. We assume that this someone produces things in answer to his or her own needs and desires. So we infer that "the Gods direct all things for the use of men in order to bind men to them and be held by men in the highest honor" (*ibid.*). We infer that gods must have given us the use of our eyes, fish-filled seas and so on in order to procure our obedience, in just the way a human king might bestow goods upon us in order to gain our allegiance. "So it has happened that each of them has thought up from his own temperament different ways of worshipping God, so that God might love them above the rest, and direct the whole of Nature according to the needs of their blind desire and insatiable greed" (*ibid.*).

"See, I ask you, how the matter has turned out in the end!" writes Spinoza.

Among so many conveniences in nature they had to find many inconveniences: storms, earthquakes, diseases, etc.

These, they maintain, happen because the Gods are angry on account of wrongs done to them by men, or on account of sins committed in their worship. And though their daily experience contradicted this, and though infinitely many examples showed that conveniences and inconveniences happen indiscriminately to the pious and impious alike, they did not on that account give up their longstanding prejudice. It was easier for them to put this among the other unknown things, whose use they were ignorant of, and so remain in the state of ignorance in which they had been born, than to destroy that whole construction, and think up a new one. (*Ibid.*)

So there are at least three errors in the making of this folk theory. The first error is in assuming that we are free agents, able to act on our own desires, because we are ignorant of the various unseen causes that move us to act. Our second error is to extend this freedom to unseen productive entities, the gods, whose psychology we assume is similar to our own. And the third error is to hold on to these beliefs in the face of all evidence to the contrary.

Thank goodness for the methods of mathematics, Spinoza says, and the style of proof it uses! When it is applied to matters of metaphysics and theology, we teach ourselves to see nature as it is, and not as we fashion it to be. And in this way we gain a more accurate appraisal of God's perfection:

[Denying necessitarianism] takes away God's perfection. For if God acts for the sake of an end, he necessarily wants something which he lacks. And though the theologians and metaphysicians distinguish between an end of need and an end of assimilation, they nevertheless confess that God did all things for his own sake, not for the sake of the things to be created. For before creation they can assign nothing except God for whose sake God would act. And so they are necessarily compelled to confess that God lacked those things for the sake of which he willed to prepare means, and that he desired them. (*Ibid.*)

If God is perfect, then there are no further ends to be obtained, no goals towards which to strive. Instead, all possible creations spill out from God's nature willy-nilly, and there can be no meaningful hope or faith about what will be. Spinoza's God is too great to be confined by any human psychology of motivation.

Spinoza's necessitarianism, I conclude, is a consequence of his reverence for the one substance's power. Any god that acted for certain ends would be a god less perfect than the one substance.

DIVINE EMANATION

We turn now to a further feature of the *how* of the one substance's generation of all possible things. To say, as I did above, that "all possible creations spill out from God's nature willy-nilly" is a crude formulation of the manner in which Spinoza's God generates modes, namely, through *divine emanation.*

"Emanation" is a technical term Spinoza inherited from scholastic metaphysics.[11] It names a kind of causality that was thought to obtain between the essence of a thing and the properties that the thing cannot fail to have. So, for example, let us suppose that the essence of a particular kind of crystal is its unique molecular structure. Inevitably, because the crystal has that unique structure, it will be able to combine with other elements, it will have a certain hardness, it will be able to undergo certain transformations, and so on. These properties of the crystal are due to, follow from, or "flow from" its essence; some scholastics would say that they *emanate* (Latin, "to flow") from that essence. Thinking of emanation as a kind of causality may seem jarring to post-Humean sensibilities, as we typically regard causality as a relation holding between events or things, and we think primarily in terms of efficient causes. But on the other hand, if someone were to ask, "What causes diamonds to be so hard?" and another were to reply, "It's a result of the crystalline structure", it would not sound like a conceptual mistake. Sometimes, the cause of a thing's property is the way that thing is.

Spinoza's claim is that all modes emanate from God, in the way the crystal's distinctive properties emanate from its essence, or "in the same way as from the nature of a triangle it follows, from eternity and to eternity, that its three angles are equal to two right angles" (*Ethics* IP17S). Of course, we already knew that Spinoza must believe something along these lines when we saw that he thought of finite things as *modes* of the one substance. But what more can be said about the view to make it better understood? How might the finite objects surrounding us and including us be thought of as features emanating from a substance?

In a recent book, Valterri Viljanen undertakes to explain Spinoza's notion of divine emanation in greater depth. He begins by pointing out that, according to Spinoza, "God's power is his essence itself" (*Ethics* IP34). Spinoza nowhere carefully articulates the relation between God's power and God's attributes, which are what the intellect conceives as pertaining to God's essence. Perhaps the attributes are different but equally adequate ways to express that essence, as the structure of a crystal might be expressed both geometrically and algebraically. At any rate, it is clear that Spinoza means to indicate that power is fundamentally *what God is* (it is "his essence *itself*"), and is not only an expression of God. *God is power*. And this will mean that the modes of God are expressions of this power.

Viljanen uses this thesis about God's essence to explain why it is, in Spinoza's metaphysics, that the one substance and all that it implies are not merely ideal entities, or entities that exist as possibles without ever becoming actual:

> [U]nlike geometrical objects that are mere beings of reason (*entia rationis*), God is a real thing, indeed the most real thing there is (*ens realissimum*) ... There is nothing outside God (IP15), and because no thing can exist without its necessary properties, we arrive at IP16 which asserts that God necessarily brings about all the properties inferable from his definition (which, in fact, means that God realizes all genuine possibilities). Now, precisely at this point – and *no earlier* – the notion of power steps in: *the realization of this necessary system of entities requires power*. In other words, because God is a real being endowed with causal power, God himself and all his properties (i.e. modifications) come to be realized.
>
> (Viljanen 2011: 62)

This captures Spinoza's metaphysical replacement for the story of Genesis: God does not decide or will anything into existence, for whatever reason or motivation; instead, God's very essence is itself the power, and this means that God and all that God's nature implies must exist.

Finite things, then, are "franchises" of God's power, local and finite expressions of a deeper and inexhaustible ontological fund. Each is constrained by infinite circumstances (as *Ethics* IP28 attests), so that each finite thing represents exactly one opportunity for God's power to be expressed in a certain and determinate way. As Viljanen puts it, in more careful and technical language, "the essences of finite things indicate the manner in which intrinsically active reality must be under a certain attribute for specific things to exist" (Viljanen 2011: 74). The particular essence of a finite thing is a specific, limiting constraint upon God's power, determining what effects that thing can have in the world.

It is illustrative to compare this interpretation of divine emanation in Spinoza's metaphysics with the concept of *being* in Paul Tillich's *Systematic Theology*. Tillich takes God to be the "being of being", or the power of being in all existent things. God does not exist in the same way finite things exist; rather, God is the ground of being for all existent things. Tillich describes God's existence in ways we have seen to be perfectly appropriate to Spinoza's one substance:

> As the power of being, God transcends every being and also the totality of beings – the world. Being-itself is beyond finitude and infinity; otherwise it would be conditioned by something other than itself, and the real power of being would lie beyond both it and that which conditioned it. Being-itself infinitely transcends every finite being. ... In calling it [being-itself] creative, we point to the fact that everything participates in the infinite power of being. (Tillich 1951: I, 237)[12]

So the being of finite things is somehow rooted in being-itself, which is God, in Tillich's view. Although Tillich goes on to develop his own theology in ways Spinoza could not possibly endorse, this fundamental thesis regarding the relation between God's existence and the existence of finite things certainly captures Spinoza's own view.

If someone approached us and wanted to know what it is to exist, we would of course be flummoxed; in desperation, we might begin by pointing at things around us in random fashion, grasping at them, and affirming existence of each and every one of them, hoping that our friend would form the conclusion that the only thing these different objects had in common was that they *exist*, and are real. It is but a short and dreamy step to move from this claim to the claim that each thing *is* existence, in a different way: the book is *existence*, book-like; the tree is *existence*, tree-like; and so on. Each is a manifestation of being. And if God is, as Tillich says, the being that is behind all beings, then he is in the company of Spinoza in claiming that all things are a manifestation or expression of God.

4

Our place in the world

I say expressly that the Mind has, not an adequate, but only a confused knowledge, of itself, of its own Body, and of external bodies, so long as it perceives things from the common order of nature. (*Ethics* IIP29S)

THE IMPORTANCE OF LOCATION

Every worldview, and so every theology, offers some sense of a place for human life: what we are, where we come from, what we should do, and where we hope to go. Many of us today hold a worldview predicated upon a scientific understanding of nature and of ourselves. As our scientific understanding develops, we get clearer ideas of where we come from and what we are and what we as human beings are likely to do. We gain an increasingly detailed knowledge of our past and present, and even our most probable futures; but what our advanced understanding lacks is any sense of *how things are supposed to be*. Of course, we can extrapolate how species, ecosystems and individuals would develop in various circumstances, and (if we want) we can call some of those circumstances "natural" or "right", but we do not find anything in nature that marks out any set of circumstances as the way things are *supposed* to be. At most we can try to determine how we *would like* things to be, and we can try to engineer policy and practice toward that particular end; but that is not quite the same as a genuine *telos*. It is preference – albeit *our* preference! – but not purpose.

Replacing a natural order with laws of nature is the early modern innovation that spelled out the legacy of the scientific revolution. The moderns shifted the Earth out of the centre of the universe, and then deprived the universe of any centre at all, and deprived humans of serving any purpose other than their own. There is both knowledge and freedom in this, to be sure; but there is also loss. If once we could say, "Here is the shape of things, and here our origin, and there our end, and so thus our life", we can say now only, "We come from there, and live like thus, and make of it what we will". Whether this will prove to be enough for us – whether we can live past our own illusions – is the great experiment we are living through today. We shall see.

Somewhere in this transition from the old order to the new indeterminacy stands Spinoza. In his conception of God he left out any place for design, purpose or natural end. In fact, he readily placed human beings in suspension between the two infinities that so haunted Pascal:

> For, in the end, what is humanity in nature? A nothing-ness, a mid-point between nothing and everything, infi-nitely far from understanding the extremes; ... equally incapable of seeing the nothingness from where he came, and the infinite in which he is covered.
>
> (*Pensées*, §230; Pascal [1669] 1995: 67)

The human being, according to Spinoza, is composed of infinitely many lesser bodies, each playing some functional role in its supe-riors, and similarly each human body plays similar functional roles in ever-larger bodies. There are no limits, large or small; we are some sort of ontological way-station between the infinitesimal and the infinite. In other words, as Spinoza himself rather sparsely declares, "Substance does not constitute the form of man" (*Ethics* IIP10).

Human beings, according to Spinoza, exist in tension between micro-forces and macro-forces. Almost all that we experience, therefore, is beyond our control. But we possess our own quantum of force as well, just as any mode of the one substance is an expression of God's power. So Spinoza is able to at least sketch what a self-governed life would be: the life a human being would naturally lead if all of those other micro- and macro-forces were silenced. Such a life is autonomous and "free" in the sense of "not constrained or compelled by others". To the extent we can arrange for our lives to approximate that ideal, we live a life that is natural to human beings, and we can look forward to the joy of self-esteem, or the knowledge that, for at least this effort at this time, we have not been merely a reactionary cog, but a prime mover in our action. In Spinoza's bleak view, that is as good as it ever gets.

And maybe that *is* as good as it gets. For we join Spinoza in seeing through the illusions that framed the golden conceit of grand purpose for human beings. The early modern dislocation has proved a permanent move. If, as we try to take seriously the purposes we set for ourselves, we could come across anything like genuine self-esteem, then that would be very nice indeed. As we shall see, there is nothing so alien in Spinoza's view of human nature as to make this impossible. We may find that the place Spinoza makes for us within an infinitely complex universe, even one in which our own force is "infinitely surpassed by the power of external causes" (*Ethics* IVP3), is a place we can recognize as both fitting and habitable, at least for the short duration of our stay.

This chapter will further articulate our place in Spinoza's cosmos. Beginning with a humbling analogy that was doubtlessly meant to dethrone any illegitimate senses of self-worth, we shall see that human lives are subject for the most part to forces beyond our knowledge and control. And yet Spinoza also maintains that there is a part of us that strives for autonomy and genuine knowledge, and – if we are fortunate – we may find ourselves in circumstances allowing for visions of the broad vistas described by the *Ethics* itself. In these vistas, it turns out (or so I shall argue) that the particulars of our lives vanish into illusion and insignificance, and we see only the eternal. In this we find a kind of immortality that (as we shall see at the end of the next chapter) can provide us with philosophical solace when the misfortunes of life threaten to overwhelm us.

First, though, a little worm.

LIKE A WORM IN THE BLOOD

In 1665, while their countries engaged in naval battles, Spinoza corresponded with the Royal Society's secretary, Henry Oldenburg, gossiping about their mutual friends, pendulums, books and telescopes, and complaining about the tendency of blood-thirsty warriors to interrupt conversations among educated people. Spinoza, for his part, confessed that he did not know whether to laugh or cry:

> For I do not think it right to laugh at nature, and far less to grieve over it, reflecting that men, like all else, are only a part of nature, and that I do not know how each part of nature harmonises with the whole, and how it coheres with other parts. And I realise that it is merely through such lack of understanding that certain features of nature – which I thus perceived only partly and in a fragmentary way, and which are not in keeping with our philosophical attitude of mind – once seemed to me vain, disordered, and absurd. But now I let everyone go his own way.
>
> (*Letters* 30, to Oldenburg)

This studied indifference ("I let everyone go his own way") gave Spinoza license to "live for the truth," that is, to focus more narrowly on what he can make sense of and let the rest of it go hang.

Spinoza's comment about parts harmonizing with the whole caught Oldenburg's attention, and (despite Spinoza's professed ignorance about it) he asked if Spinoza could cast any more light on the subject. In reply, Spinoza insisted that he did not have any detailed knowledge, but that he could at least provide his grounds for thinking that there has to be such harmony among the parts of the world. He first explained what he meant by *harmony* or *coherence of parts*: it is when the parts of a larger entity coordinate their behaviours and actions with one another so that there is the least degree of conflict among them. Their actions cohere with one another, as much as possible. In fact he does not make good on his promise, and does not explain to Oldenburg exactly *why* he thinks that everything has to cohere in this way. He merely asserts that "all bodies are surrounded by others and are reciprocally determined to exist and to act in a fixed and determinate way, the same ratio of motion and rest being preserved in them taken all together": language that mirrors what he says in a digression just following *Ethics* IIP13, where (as we saw in the previous chapter) he describes the great big Individual consisting of all of the bodies in the universe (the "face" of the whole universe).

But, Spinoza points out, even if we are sure *that* all bodies must cohere and harmonize in this way, we still are completely ignorant about the *nature* of that harmony: what makes it happen, and what polices it. And he offers a humbling analogy to make his point. Spinoza compares our plight to that of a worm living in someone's blood, a worm that is:

> capable of distinguishing by sight the particles of blood – lymph, etc. – and of intelligently observing how each particle, on colliding with another, either rebounds or communicates some degree of motion, and so forth. That worm would be living in the blood as we are living in our part of the universe, and it would regard each individual particle of the blood as a whole, not a part, and it could have no idea as to how all the parts are controlled by the overall nature of the blood and compelled to mutual adaptation as the overall nature of the blood requires, so as to agree with one another in a definite way.
>
> (*Letters* 32, to Oldenburg)

The worm can see and understand local events at its own scale, but cannot see how these events fit into the larger scheme of things. Spinoza offers the anatomical analogy because he was no doubt convinced that human bodies regulate themselves in some holistic fashion, where smaller parts behave as they do in fulfilment of the larger organism's requirements. The little worm would know nothing of this. So, as we are in an epistemic position analogous to the worm's, we see navies colliding, men dying and all attending calamities without understanding how these events play their roles within a larger natural system, and are even required by that system to be as they are. We see only the effects, and not the broader causality at work. A more powerful order of nature, which we do not fully comprehend, results in events that strike us as merely chaotic, confused and violent.

In the same letter, Spinoza says a little more in order to make his point about nature's harmony explicit:

> All bodies are surrounded by others and are reciprocally determined to exist and to act in a fixed and determinate way, the same ratio of motion and rest being preserved in them all taken together, that is, in the universe as a whole. Hence it follows that every body, in so far as it exists as modified in a definite way, must be considered as a part of the whole universe, and as agreeing with the whole and cohering with the other parts. (*Letters* 32, to Oldenburg)

So Spinoza believes there are some unseen forces at work in the determination of bodies' motions: namely, forces stemming from the overall nature of the corporeal universe. This universal nature of the universe plays an active role in regulating the behaviour of bodies. As a result, reductionistic laws of impact are simply not enough for understanding why finite individuals behave as they do. We need also to know that there are other global forces at work, acting to control and adjust the motions of bodies when they collide. This does not make the resulting physical worldview any less deterministic, but it does indicate that Spinoza's universe has the behaviour of its parts resulting at least in part from the nature of the whole, and this sets him apart from other prominent determinists of his time.

Spinoza might even say that we, in our wormish ignorance, are usually unable to see how events fit into "God's overall plan", though he would wince and fidget as he said so. For, as he explains earlier in the letter to Oldenburg, "I do not attribute to Nature beauty, ugliness, order or confusion", and surely the same goes for goodness, justice and mercy. "God's plan" for Spinoza at most can mean only the way the universe maintains its constancy over time through laws of conservation. It is not so much a plan as it is a policy without exceptions.

GROWTH AND JOY; SADNESS AND AGE

But at some point the larger forces whose metabolic needs we unwittingly serve will meet with the quantum of force that is us. Spinoza attributes to each of us, as well as to all individuals, an "actual essence" to strive to persevere in existing (*Ethics* IIIP7). This striving to persevere – or, in Latin, our *conatus* – is what unifies us with the one substance, whose own actual essence is also the raw power to be. As we saw at the end of the previous chapter, in saying we are modes of one substance, Spinoza is saying that our strivings to be are modes of the grand universal power to exist, or God's essence itself (*Ethics* IP34).

Having a *conatus* means that we are not merely passive, and we are not completely indifferent to whatever changes the world thrusts upon us. We resist certain changes, in so far as we are able, and we seek out those influences that are conducive to our *conatus*, and we resent, hate and avoid anything that acts in opposition to it. From this basic, unalterable disposition on our part we derive the two fundamental emotional states in Spinoza's account of the human being. *Joy* is the experience of something conducive to our *conatus*, and *pain* (or sorrow, sadness, or depression – basically, the general feeling of being oppressed by circumstances contrary to our advantage) is the experience of anything opposed to our *conatus*. The dominance of one or the other of those two emotions serves as a general weather vane to indicate, in general, how things are going for us in our lifelong battle against those forces in nature that surpass us infinitely in power.[1] At any moment we are in ascent, or in decline.

We shall begin by focusing on what brings us joy. Persevering, according to Spinoza, means maintaining one's own nature, or one's own systematic functioning. "Systematic functioning" here replaces what Spinoza calls an individual's *ratio* of motion and rest. He uses this term to mean a general pattern of functioning, and it is precisely this that individuates bodies from one another and marks them off from the plenum of extended matter in which they reside. For matter is all the same, according to Spinoza: it is extended stuff. The only way to set some of it apart from the rest is to introduce into it a distinctive *swirl*, or some complex pattern of motion among its components. The Latin term *"ratio"* could mean a mathematical ratio, but it can also mean simply a pattern (as well, of course, as several other things that are not relevant here). The general point Spinoza is making is that to maintain a body over time is to ensure that a pattern of motion is maintained; the parts may come and go, so long as they stay in the same stable swirl of motion with respect to one another, like a swarm, a mob or a system of planets. That systematic functioning is the individual's *form*, or *nature*, and the individual's *conatus* is its striving to retain that form or nature for as long as possible.

Joy is what we experience when we enjoy greater success in maintaining our form. Health, good nutrition, the rewards of exercise, strength and flexibility all bring joy to us, as by them we grow in strength. Spinoza, in fact, provides a refreshing list of all the things in which a wise and happy person should participate, a list that shows he is no stern figure of puritanical stripe:

> It is the part of a wise man, I say, to refresh and restore himself in moderation with pleasant food and drink, with scents, with the beauty of green plants, with decoration, music, sports, the theater, and other things of this kind, which anyone can use without injury to one another. For the human body is composed of a great many parts of different natures, which constantly require new and varied nourishment, so that the whole body may be equally capable of all the things which can follow from its nature.
>
> (*Ethics* IVP45S)

Moderate engagement with the varied pleasures of the world nourishes us and makes us capable of greater action. Moreover, this is *why* such engagement brings us joy: joy simply is the experience of greater capability, or greater power to sustain oneself and one's activity. That which stimulates us makes us stronger.

A similar kind of account can be given for Spinozistic sadness. Just as we encounter things that strengthen us and cause us to feel joy, we encounter other things that decrease our abilities to act and so cause us to be sad, depressed or sick. These things diminish our powers to maintain ourselves over time. The account of sadness is parallel to that of joy, with the arrows pointed in the opposite direction. Indeed, the two have an inverse relation, such that the loss of a joy is experienced as sadness, and the loss of a cause for sadness is itself a joy.

Over our lives, it seems that Spinoza must maintain that we eventually begin to experience a greater proportion of sadness-inducing things than joy-inducing ones, for once we reach maturity it is evident that we begin to age, weaken and die. So far as I can see, Spinoza has no other means for accounting for the process of aging; he has no internal spring that eventually winds down, no natural decline in the body's ability to repair broken cells. Indeed, he demonstrates that it is impossible for a body to contain within itself the seeds for its own destruction ("No thing can be destroyed except through an external cause"; *Ethics* IIIP4).[2] Our aging must, then, result from increased friction with our environment. Why it always happens, and at roughly the same time across individuals' lives, remains something of a mystery, on Spinoza's account of things.

VIRTUOUS MINDS AND BODIES

Thus, according to Spinoza, we seek by nature that which meets the needs of our nature, and shun all else. Another way of putting this is that we are by nature *virtuous*, at least according to Spinoza's understanding of "virtue". "The striving to preserve oneself is the first and only foundation of virtue" (*Ethics* IVP22C), he claims with the utmost confidence. So virtue, for Spinoza, is first and foremost a matter of meeting our own existential demands, specifically what we demand for strength in self-preservation. But this definition of virtue does not lead to results as counter-intuitive as it may at first seem. For, first of all, people can become quite confused about what best meets their needs for self-preservation, so we will find people engaged in foolish and destructive activity that does not count as virtuous, although the destructive fools may deem it so. Moreover, it will turn out that forming a strongly cooperative community with others will turn out to be extremely valuable in securing our own survival, so our dedication to our own self-preservation will result in many actions typically seen as virtuous, even aside from Spinoza's definition. But he is absolutely straightforward about basing the true morality upon a foundation of self-interest.

Joy, as we have identified it, has to do with meeting the body's demands, and enhancing its capacities and strengths. The mind, according to Spinoza, is the idea of the body, so there should be a recognizably parallel account of what registers as joy and virtue for the mind. And for the most part, with an exception to be explained shortly, this is so. The mind is a collection of ideas and images, striving to maintain its characteristic organization over time. A great many of these ideas and images are composites representing both the body itself and external bodies coming into causal contact with it. So what counts as health and strength for the body coincides with what counts as health and strength for the mind:

> I say this in general, that in proportion as a body is more capable than others of doing many things at once, or being acted on in many ways at once, so its mind is more capable than others of perceiving many things at once. And in proportion as the actions of the body depend more on itself alone, and as other bodies concur with it less in acting, so its mind is more capable of understanding distinctly.
>
> (*Ethics* IIP13S)

Sensitivity and capability in mind and body come hand in hand, so to speak, or not at all. Of course, one is tempted to draw up counter-examples of ignorant gymnasts or clumsy geniuses. But these counter-examples are too crude, because bodies and minds have so many different kinds of sensitivities and capacities. The gymnast has greater cognitive awareness of balance and a much clearer understanding of (let us call it) the domain of gymnastic possibilities. The genius's brain has a kind of operational strength that leaves the rest of us far behind. Some parts of the body will figure more prominently than others when it comes to the specific kinds of mental abilities we are interested in; and similarly, each mental ability will be paired with a physical capacity that may not be obvious at first glance. The fact that thick biceps do not always correlate with a fascination for cryptograms should not trouble us; we share Spinoza's recognition that differences in mental abilities are grounded in something physical, just as physical abilities bring with them special kinds of information-processing.

So, generally, the accounts of the body's striving and the mind's striving for self-preservation will run in harness. But there is one part of the mind that is exceptional on Spinoza's account: *reason*, or our capacity to frame adequate ideas. Spinoza's bare-boned accounting for this fact is as follows. Many of the ideas constituting our mind are ideas of idiosyncratic parts or features of our bodies. But some of the ideas are of features our bodies share with all bodies, namely, basic geometrical and physical features. These ideas of features common to all bodies form the foundation of reason, according to Spinoza, and he calls them "common notions" because they are ideas of features common to all bodies (*Ethics* IIP38–P40). The ideas of reason, although simple and few, are sufficient for generating a world unto themselves. An idea of a point and the idea of motion produces an idea of a line; fixing one end of the line and revolving the other end around it produces the idea of a circle; rotating the circle about its axis produces a sphere; and so on, and on, until we have all the geometrical furniture necessary for recreating Descartes' *World*. The common notions enable us to form a mathematical model of anything in the world and thus attain a clear and distinct understanding of it.[3]

This part of the mind, reason, has a striving notably different from the striving of the body or the striving of the mind as a whole. They all seek self-preservation, but reason strives after understanding. Perhaps it would be right to say (although Spinoza does not) that reason, like an individual body or mind, strives after its own greater strength, which translates into an ever broader and clearer understanding of all things. Pursuing understanding is the mind's greatest good: "the mind, insofar as it reasons, cannot conceive anything to be good for itself except what leads to understanding" (*Ethics* IVP26D). And since this is in truth ("insofar as it reasons") the mind's greatest good, it yields a great satisfaction, which Spinoza identifies as the strongest subspecies of "self esteem". He explains this in his demonstration of *Ethics* IVP52 (modified slightly here for ease of reading):

> Self-esteem is a joy born of the fact that man considers himself and his power of acting. But man's true power of acting, or virtue, is reason itself. Therefore, self-esteem arises from reason. Moreover, while a man considers himself, he perceives nothing clearly and distinctly, or adequately, except those things which follow from his power of acting, that is, which follow from his power of understanding. And so the greatest self-esteem there can be arises only from this reflection, q.e.d.
>
> *Scholium*: Self-esteem is really the highest thing we can hope for ...

Spinoza locates here what he believes to be our greatest self-initiated activity, and our highest joy: the mind's capacity to understand through reason. But, interestingly, this self-initiated enquiry stands to the side of what he has identified as the body's and the mind's strivings towards self-preservation. The body and mind strive for their own preservation; meanwhile, reason, an important subset (or aspect or capacity) of the mind, has its own brand of striving, and its success yields in fact "the highest thing we can hope for", which is self-esteem, or the impersonal joy of rational enlightenment. So it turns out that the preservation for the individual as a whole is not the highest thing we can hope for. That may be because we should know by this point that any such hope will be quashed. On the other hand, the hope for the triumph of reason – its final self-preservation – will be fulfilled with all necessity, as we shall see.

PASSIVITY AND ILLUSION

If the whole of nature were attuned to our own *conatus*, life would be nothing but continuous mental and physical improvement and the triumph of rational enlightenment. But, alas, there are complications.

We are constantly getting pushed around, sometimes gently, and other times not so gently. Most saliently, we are pushed around as light enters our eyes, pressure waves assault skin and ears, and molecules collide with tongues and nostrils. All of these external attacks upon our person register in our minds as *images*, meaning "representations of the impinging force". As we should have learned at school, really there are no colours or sounds or smells independent of the observer; there are only physical changes and motions in the natural world and in our bodily organs themselves, which come to be observed by us as colours or sounds or smells.

Our faculty for turning impinging forces into representation is the *imagination*, and Spinoza regards it as a clearly inferior source of knowledge. The basic problem with the imagination is that each representation it constructs is a blended representation of something going on outside us with something going on inside us. Each image is thus a *confusion*, and it is very difficult for us to tease apart what is external from what is internal. Consequently, it is very difficult to get an accurate representation of anything by using the imagination. The imagination is able to tell us, at the very least, that there is *something* going on external to us, although, of course, it may not be at all what we think it is. Indeed, Spinoza demonstrates that a representation gained through the imagination never yields adequate knowledge of an external body (*Ethics* IIP25).

The world, then, is not as it appears to be. This moral is nothing new; who has ever thought otherwise? What is distinctive is Spinoza's account of how we come to know what the world really is. The real world is the one disclosed to us through conceptual demonstrations and deductive apparatus such as that deployed in the *Ethics*. It is a world of eternal geometrical truths, of concepts as they are arranged in the intellect of God. We can gain access to this world only rarely, for it requires that the din of the external world is silenced and our reason is determined by its own *conatus*, which strives to understand ideas and bestow upon us self-esteem. Being inwardly determined by reason is the only way to have adequate knowledge of anything:

> I say expressly that the mind has, not an adequate, but only a confused knowledge, of itself, of its own body, and of external bodies, so long as it perceives things from the common order of Nature, that is, so long as it is determined externally, from fortuitous encounters with things, to regard this or that, and not so long as it is determined internally, from the fact that it regards a number of things at once, to understand their agreements, differences, and oppositions. (*Ethics* IIP29S)

This might seem odd at first: why should we think that, so far as the mind is insulated from external disturbances, it will gain adequate ideas but, to the extent that it observes and is affected by external objects, it will have only inadequate knowledge? Normally we think just the opposite is true: if you want adequate knowledge of the world around you, you should start with careful observation!

But on further reflection, it is certainly true that anyone who *only* observes will have no knowledge. Observations are useful to the extent they inform a *theory*, which by its very nature reaches beyond all observations. And, given Spinoza's necessitarianism (than which none greater can be conceived), any theory that is true must be necessarily true. In other words, no theory is founded ultimately on contingent or brute facts known through observation, according to Spinoza. Each theory is grounded in necessary truths. If we somehow arrive at a theory that is in fact true, but we have not seen through to its necessity, then Spinoza would regard our knowledge of that theory as inadequate. If, on the other hand, we truly do have adequate knowledge of a theory, then we must see and understand its necessity. Only reason will show us the necessity of a truth. Therefore, all adequate knowledge comes from within, in so far as the mind is active in determining its own ideas. Knowledge based upon our passivity, or our receptivity to being moved by objects external to us, can be only inadequate.

This last point can stand to be amplified a bit. From the perspective of reason's own striving for adequate knowledge, events that generate imaginative models of the world – call them "epistemic collisions" – count as injuries. Nothing adequate comes of the imagination. It is only when the mind is secured from outside influences that consequences can be validly inferred from innate common notions, and adequate knowledge can be achieved. Metaphysics is done best, and most safely, from the armchair.

THE ILLUSORY NATURE OF ORDINARY EXPERIENCE

The fact that the world as we ordinarily perceive it is in fact a confused and inadequate representation of the real, and the real world is best represented by concepts constructed purely from autonomous reason, raises the question of whether ordinary experience is an illusion. Consider this. As Spinoza demonstrates, the only way we know that we have a body in the first place, or indeed that there are any bodies at all in the universe, is through the "affections" – that is, through the imagination (*Ethics* IIPP19 & 26). But we have seen that the imagination yields only inadequate and confused ideas. What confidence should we have, then, that we have bodies, or that we are surrounded by bodies?

Spinoza does take pains to point out that our ordinary perception of things in the world does not provide a true model of the actual existence of those things. In commenting on a proposition that claims that the idea of each thing "involves an eternal and infinite essence of God" (IIP45S), Spinoza clarifies what he means by "existence":

> By existence I do not understand duration, that is, existence insofar as it is conceived abstractly, and as a certain species of quantity. For I am speaking of the very nature of existence, which is attributed to singular things because infinitely many things follow from the eternal necessity of God's nature in infinitely many modes. I am speaking, I say, of the very existence of singular things insofar as they are in God. (*Ethics* IIP45S)

The natural reading of this passage is that "the very nature of existence" or "the very existence of singular things" is itself eternal, as the existence of the one substance is eternal. Ultimately, bodies are their geometrical forms, as timeless as any mathematical objects, and their ideas are pure concepts in the intellect of the one substance. What shall we say, then, about the sort of existence our experience presents singular things as having, in so far as they change or endure through some portion of time? Again, this passage suggests that such existence is conceived *abstractly* and (to employ the adjective Spinoza often pairs with it) *inadequately*. This seems to indicate that the durational existence of things is at least *somewhat* illusory, or at any rate not as adequately conceived as the "very nature" of their existence, which is itself eternal.

Some commentators might feel a need to rescue Spinoza from this conclusion that the world of material objects enduring through time is not as fully real as reality gets. But in fact Spinoza cannot resist this conclusion, and he gives no evidence of wishing to do so. There can be no doubt that the only substance in existence, on his view, is changeless and eternal; there can also be no doubt that each singular thing *is* that one substance, modified in some determinate way. From the perspective of some singular thing, it will *look as if* there is time and change; but this is necessarily a limited perspective and an inadequate representation of the true natures of things. The view *sub specie aeternitatis*, or "from an eternal perspective", is the view that gets things right.

Recall that Spinoza wrote in his letter to Oldenburg that "it is merely through such lack of understanding that certain features of nature – which I thus perceived only partly and in a fragmentary way, and which are not in keeping with our philosophical attitude of mind – once seemed to me vain, disordered, and absurd" (*Letters* 30, to Oldenburg). Earlier we saw one motivation for believing this, arising from the insight that we do not know any more about the universe's workings than a parasitical worm does about the functioning of a host's body. But now we see a second motivation arising from the recognition that the world is not at all as it appears to our senses. Everything that would make a sea battle so fearsome is, in truth, some distortion of reality, which is geometrical, changeless, eternal. If we let "the dead bury the dead", that is, if we leave appearances to look after themselves, and if we choose instead "to live for the truth", as Spinoza announces as his own intention, then we will turn aside from the vain, disordered and absurd world of appearances and look instead towards the geometrical world of the changeless intellect. We will swap the perspective of time-bound beings for an eternal perspective.

In the next two sections I shall offer brief accounts of Spinoza's psychotherapy, which is his advice for separating one's thoughts from the world as it is modelled by the imagination, and of Spinoza's doctrine of the eternity of the rational part of the mind. Then, with these accounts in hand, we can return again to the question of whether the ordinary world is an illusion, according to Spinoza. I shall argue that one of Spinoza's later followers, Salomon Maimon (1753–1800), was right to see in Spinoza's philosophy a strong inclination toward acosmism, or the denial of the existence of the particulars of experience.

CURING LIFE WITH REASON: SPINOZA'S PSYCHOTHERAPY

Swapping the timely perspective for an eternal one is the key to Spinoza's psychotherapy, or his advice for how one should live, given that our bodily and cognitive autonomy is under constant assault. Very often, his advice will be of no use at all, since we operate under the sway of sensations or emotions or stimuli that overwhelm us, or at any rate distract our cognitive powers from their own natural *conatus*. But sometimes we may be so fortunate as to be able to direct our thoughts and our behaviour on our own terms, that is, according to our innermost strivings.

In such cases, our mind's striving for rational understanding will cause us to try to understand what the true causes of our experience are, and to try to distinguish external events from internal ones. By nature our minds strive to understand through reason; when we are not overwhelmed, this is what we will naturally try to do. In so far as we succeed, we will form adequate ideas or models of our own internal states and the states of the outside world. Immediately, all of the emotions tied up with our confused states will disappear: for *almost* all emotions arise from the imagination, and therefore from inadequate ideas. ("*Almost*", because we must set aside the cognitive joy that arises in us when our reason succeeds and we recognize ourselves as the cause of our own strength; that is the joy of self-esteem, and it does not arise from the imagination.) The ideas we build up through reason, and through the common notions, are more powerful than imaginative ideas and they will eventually replace them. Through reason we gain a clear and sober assessment of the emotional or imaginative states we are in (or rather, the states we *were* in), and in so doing we exit those states and experience a distinctly rational joy that arises from the use of our own rational powers. This brand of independence from imaginative affects Spinoza identifies as "human freedom", and part V of the *Ethics* is dedicated to it.

In providing this therapy for the passions, it is noteworthy that Spinoza cannot be understood as giving advice that we may either freely accept or freely reject as we see fit. For that conception of advice-giving presupposes a kind of deliberative freedom that we do not have, on Spinoza's account. Instead, he is only charting causal consequences from a neutral point of view. One sees, from this neutral view, that when human beings are in a state free of disturbance and interruption, they will begin to parse the world and themselves through the instruments of reason, and they will enjoy the resultant pleasure of self-esteem.[4] No doubt, there are many obstacles that keep human beings from following this natural inclination: there are not only neighbours shouting, kettles boiling and dogs barking, but there are also desires we humans have acquired that propel us towards other involvements, endeavours, daydreams and fantasies. So the fact that, as you may recall, the last time you had some free time you did not begin constructing representations out of common notions, does not immediately nullify Spinoza's account. You were on that occasion distracted by something, represented by your imagination, and your focus of attention was not as free from disturbance as you may have believed.

Still, Spinoza's documentation of the emotional geometry of human psychology (*Ethics* III, preface) – in short, his writing down this apparent advice and our reading it – *itself* exerts some causal effect upon us, one that could conceivably influence our thoughts and behaviour under the right conditions. He is determined to write the words that will causally influence us to behave in one way or another. Moreover, as we shall see in the next chapter, he believes himself to be motivated to influence our behaviour by forces arising from his own *conatus*: his own desire for self-preservation causes him to try to get others to be determined by their own *conatus*. In this sense, Spinoza is trying to persuade us, or attempting to modify behaviour, even if he disavows the sort of freedom that "advice" is normally thought to presuppose.

Spinoza deduces many details about affective states and ideas achieved through reason, and the struggle among them, but it is the overall character of this therapy that we shall focus on. Our engagement with the world of emotions, of the senses, of our daily pains and pleasures, is predicated upon passivity and illusion. Our getting pushed and pulled by the world is often a case of failure or slavery from the perspective of our *conatus* (unless we are lucky and the pushing and pulling is in the same direction as our *conatus* directs; but let us not count on that). It is only when we can silence the forces of the outer world, or artfully align them against one another in some sort of "equal and opposite" fashion, that we can enter into a state of self-determination and self-incurred joy, which is (again) "the highest thing we can hope for". In this Spinoza shows his rationalism and his stoicism. An important philosophical source for both of these doctrines is a fundamental distrust of what fortune throws our way. It is far better, these doctrines maintain, to find a sort of joy that cannot be stolen or disrupted than to trust in luck, even if the pursuit of that joy in some sense alienates you from your surroundings.

This orientation is movingly expressed in the beginning of Spinoza's *Treatise on the Emendation of the Intellect*, where he writes:

> After experience had taught me that all the things which regularly occur in ordinary life are empty and futile, ... I resolved at last to try to find out whether there was anything which would be the true good, capable of communicating itself, and which alone would affect the mind, all others being rejected – whether there was something which, once found and acquired, would continuously give me the greatest joy to eternity. (§1; Curley, 7)

The fact that a joy does not last condemns it, in this view. We have seen that Spinoza is no ascetic, and he recommends the varied pleasurable activities of life. But he recommends them only to the extent that they develop the flexibility and strength of mind and body, which should lead in the end to a greater cultivation of reason and autonomy. Worldly pleasures are instrumentally valuable, training us for the rational joy of understanding. He is no ascetic, but he also is no Falstaff. The highest thing we can hope for is the feeling that we have achieved some kind of transcendence over the pushing and pulling of ordinary things and have seen through to the essence of the world.

Indeed, in the greatest act of transcendence Spinoza offers, we transcend even ourselves.

THE ETERNITY OF THE MIND

Spinoza, as we have seen, regards the mind and the body as one and the same thing, conceived through different attributes. Experience strongly suggests that all bodies decay; one would presume then that, if the mind is the same thing as the body, then it must undergo its own form of decay or disintegration, and thus there can be no immortality in Spinoza's philosophy.

But this conclusion is drawn too quickly. We have just seen that the changing, decaying world represented through our imaginations is not an adequate representation of the true nature of things, which is eternal and changeless within the resources of the one substance. The schematics or blueprints for all possible things reside eternally in God. The things' coming into being and going out the other way are only the representations of a confused and inadequate faculty. So there is room after all for some kind of immortality.

Of course, the immortality Spinoza describes in part V of the *Ethics* is nothing like immortality as it is commonly *imagined*. Truly eternal or timeless existence is by its nature beyond the reach of the imagination. But it is not beyond the reach of the intellect, or reason's power to demonstrate truths:

And though it is impossible that we should recollect that we existed before the body – since there cannot be any traces of this in the body, and eternity can neither be defined by time nor have any relation to time – still, we feel and know by experience that we are eternal. For the mind feels those things that it conceives in understanding no less than those it has in the memory. For the eyes of the mind, by which it sees and observes things, are the demonstrations themselves. (*Ethics* VP23S)

These remarks follow a proposition in which Spinoza declares that "the human mind cannot be absolutely destroyed with the body, but something of it remains which is eternal" (*Ethics* VP23). The peculiar phrase "something of it remains" (or the phrase used in the demonstration, "something pertains to the essence of the human mind") recalls the language of *Ethics* IVP36S, where Spinoza writes that "it pertains to the essence of the human mind to have an adequate knowledge of God's eternal and infinite essence". In this context he is writing about *reason*.[5] So the human mind as a whole is not eternal or immortal. This we should have already guessed, because so much of the mind is polluted by inadequate ideas and confused images. What survives is what has always been: ideas born of pure reason, constituents both of God's essence and our own.

It is interesting that in *Ethics* VP23S Spinoza writes that "there cannot be any traces" of this eternal part of us in the body. He certainly is ruling out any *memory* we might have of eternal existence, since memory, like the imagination, is physiologically encoded. This eternal part is apparently some element in the mind that is not linked to some individual feature of the body (like a neural structure). Nevertheless, "we feel and know by experience that we are eternal". When we formulate demonstrations and discover connections among concepts, it is *not like nothing* to be us. We experience the construction of those demonstrations and the flashes of insight to which we are drawn. But these "Aha!" moments may not be what Spinoza has in mind. Instead, when we demonstrate, for example, that substances cannot share attributes, that item of adequate knowledge becomes part of our cognitive structure, and the experience of that idea's new "residency" may be what Spinoza has in mind. We have whatever experience it is to entertain an adequate idea. The eyes of the mind are the demonstrations themselves, we are told, so presumably the "visual datum" of the mind's eyes are the demonstrations' conclusions. Being aware of an eternal truth is feeling and knowing by experience that we are eternal.

Needless to say, to those longing for immortality, this is about as exciting as discovering that people long before us and long after us have agreed and will continue to agree that two plus two equals four, and that triangles have three sides. It is completely impersonal. But that is the point. To wish for personal immortality is to be in bondage to the world as represented by the imagination. Our greatest striving, and our greatest joy, is to understand the world *sub specie aeternitatis*, or from the perspective of the one substance itself. Gaining adequate ideas, according to Spinoza, is recognizing our true natures as modes of an eternal, unchanging substance. To put the point paradoxically, finding ourselves means transcending ourselves. Instead of identifying ourselves with the collection of representations offered through the imagination, we identify ourselves with the ideas of the intellect, that is, with the mind of God.

The joy experienced as we lose ourselves in this way is the rational joy of self-esteem. That might sound impossible because the self is precisely what is getting lost in this process. But the self is not getting lost so much as gaining the adequate idea of itself as a mode of God. Thus the experienced joy is associated with the one substance as both cause and object. At root, it is the one substance enjoying its growing capacity to recognize itself. Or, as Spinoza understands the terms, "The mind's intellectual love of God is the very love of God by which God loves himself ...; that is, the mind's intellectual love of God is part of the infinite love by which God loves himself" (*Ethics* VP36).

Ultimately, a mind can be nothing other than a constellation of ideas, brought into a kind of functional unity through a certain *conatus*. But ideas are not like atoms. They can be merged, or confused; moreover, ideas *represent* other ideas or things, and can do so with clarity or obscurity. At the ultimate level of reality in Spinoza's metaphysics, of course, there are no confused, inadequate or obscure ideas. These imperfections, like mirages, only *seem* to be there, particularly to finite collections of ideas that lack certain key ideas. And thus *we* ourselves, as we ordinarily conceive ourselves, only *seem* to be here. As we take up certain key ideas, such as the ones advanced in Spinoza's *Ethics*, we gain an increasingly adequate picture of a universe that, at its deepest level, does not contain us. It is in this final act of subtraction that the rationalist, or the stoic, or the Buddhist, puts the world finally into focus, and most fully realizes that all the earthly business that might have seemed "vain, disordered, and absurd" is in fact nothing to worry about.[6]

SPINOZA THE ACOSMIST?

We can now return to the question of to what extent Spinoza saw our familiar world of finite things as an illusion. Such a view can be called "acosmism". An acosmist is someone who denies the existence of the cosmos, or nature, just as an "atheist" is someone who denies the existence of God. At least one devoted eighteenth-century student of Spinoza, Salomon Maimon, believed that in the end Spinoza's substance monism leads to acosmism.[7] It is worth pursuing this line of thought, since we have just seen that there is a strong sense in which we, at least as we ordinarily conceive ourselves, do not fully exist on Spinoza's final account; moreover, the argument could be extended to any finite thing.

Maimon began his philosophical career with an objection to Kant's philosophy. He argued that Kant, *pace* the Transcendental Deduction, had no right simply to presume that the concepts of the understanding would be at all applicable to sensory experience. We can put his objection in more general terms. Any science or any theoretical philosophy begins with the presumption that the necessities we discover through our own intellects will be mirrored in any world that exists independently of us. It is very hard to see how anyone, including Kant, could supply a rational argument in support of this presumption, since any such argument would presume exactly what it is setting out to prove, namely, that rational arguments have some purchase on reality. Maimon then offers a possible resolution of this difficulty, which is idealism. His line of thought was to base all our understanding on the structure of the mind itself, so that we would not have to worry about how some extra-mental reality connected with the concepts of our intellect. But this intellect, of course, would have to be rich enough to supply everything we could possibly come to know. An infinite intellect such as that traditionally ascribed to God, Maimon proposed, fits this bill exactly, because it would contain within itself a complete understanding of all reality, but would remain by its nature thoroughly conceptual.

And this invocation of God's intellect drives Maimon's philosophy towards Spinozism. Maimon held there to be a single substance, an infinite intellect, which carries within itself the resources for generating the concepts of all possible things, including the things that (somehow, probably though our own limitations and shortcomings) end up appearing to us as material, spatiotemporal individuals. Each apparent finite thing is only an expression of this infinite intellect, or some kind of limited and distorted version of it. But these finite individuals remain forever problematic, on Maimon's view. For we are able to conceive them as finite and spatiotemporal only because we misunderstand them; in other words, if our understanding were entirely accurate, we would not know of any finite things in space and time, but only the contents of the infinite intellect. While Maimon thought we can continually improve our intellects, and thus draw closer to the mind of God, he believed that our nature necessarily precludes us from ever acquiring perfect knowledge. For consider: we are finite individuals. And this means we ourselves do not really exist, except as limitations of the infinite intellect. And that infinite intellect has been perfect in its understanding from all eternity, as the saying goes. In the end, there really is only thought thinking infinite thought, eternally, and any partial advancements we finite and durational entities appear to make in our understanding will in the end turn out to be just that: partial and apparent.

Of course, unlike Maimon, Spinoza did not seem to have any qualms about building genuine extension into the nature of reality; he names it as an attribute of God, after all. But Maimon would apply some familiar pressure to this claim. For, as we all know, it is *the intellect* that perceives Extension as belonging to the nature of the one substance; and again, the difference between a mode conceived as extended and the same mode conceived as thinking is a distinction made by *the intellect*, and is thus (it seems) a distinction of reason. So the entities falling under these attributes are not really distinct at all, except in so far as the intellect makes them so.[8] In any event, there are enough tensions in this area to provide further support for thinking that Spinoza is, in the end, whether he would like it or not, committed to some form of idealism.

Spinoza should also be open to the particular kind of scepticism that Maimon advanced. For consider what we have seen in *Ethics* V. Our intellect's knowledge of the one substance is the very same knowledge with which the one substance knows itself, at least to the extent that our intellect is conceived *sub specie aeternitatis* (*Ethics* VP36), which (as we have already seen) is "the very existence" of any finite mode. That is, when we remove the mere abstractions of space and time, and focus on our intellects *sub specie aeternitatis*, what we find is that our intellect's representations are one and the same with those found in an infinite intellect. But then we might wonder: how exactly are our intellects, so rightly conceived, in any way distinct from the infinite intellect? And the answer quite apparently is that they are not; that, again, as with Maimon, we are left in the end with nothing but thought thinking infinite thought, eternally. And any appearance of anything other than that must be limited, illusory or distorted.

Of course, this conclusion would push Spinoza's philosophy beyond any kind of idealism and into a full-blown acosmism. For everything said here about the human mind applies equally well to all finite individuals: namely, that none of them are genuinely real, upon an adequate understanding of reality. Their existence is predicated upon the limitations and distortions of any finite intellect. Emend the intellect, and the whole world vanishes. All that is left is an eternal substance, its eternal attributes, and its infinite and eternal modes. The finite individuals showing up in *Ethics* IP28 are the individuals that can never be legitimately generated, and exist only as entities of the imagination.

In this, as in so many things, Leibniz was prescient. In 1714, writing to Louis Bourguet, he argued that his postulation of monads saved him from falling into Spinozism:

> [I]t is through these very monads that Spinozism is destroyed, for there are just as many true substances, as many living mirrors of the universe which subsist always, or as many concentrated universes, as there are monads;

105

according to Spinoza, on the contrary, there is only one substance. *He would be right if there were no monads; then everything except God would be a passing nature and would vanish into simple accidents or modifications, since there would be no substantial foundation in things, such as consist in the existence of monads.*

(Leibniz/Loemker, 663, emphasis added)

By attributing to monads some measure of independent existence, Leibniz keeps them distinct from God, thus saving us from collapsing into him and him from being stained by us.[9]

CONCLUSION

Maimon may be right or wrong in inferring these conclusions from Spinoza's system, but it is undeniable that the system leans dramatically toward acosmism. At the same time it is undeniable that Spinoza himself took finite individuals as quite real, as his ethics and political philosophy would be so much nonsense if he did not. It is as if Spinoza had opposed philosophical inclinations, one taking him in the direction of pure rationalism and stoicism, and the other in a more nominalistic and more politically engaged affirmation of the here and now. The great scholar Leszek Kołakowski identified these opposing inclinations as the two faces of Spinoza, or "the two eyes of his thought":

one directing its escapist gaze towards the all-encompassing power of the Absolute, the other concentrating it on the world of finite things, observed with the dispassionate rationalism of the scientist. One eye belongs to the apostle of deductive reasoning, the follower of Euclid, the rationalist who attempted, and failed, to construct his metaphysics on Euclidean principles; the other belongs to the mystic.

(Kołakowski 2004: 13)

But I disagree with Kołakowski's characterization of the two eyes. I think the mystical eye was also the Euclidean one, and Spinoza's acosmism was both thoroughly rationalistic and geometrical. The other eye, the one trained on finite objects, is better described as one inherited from Machiavelli and Hobbes. We turn to the world surveyed by this eye in the next chapter.

5

Spinoza's republic

Now if human nature were so constituted that men desired most of all what was most to their advantage, no special skill would be needed to secure harmony and trust. But since, admittedly, human nature is far otherwise constituted, the state must necessarily be so established that all men, both rulers and ruled, whether they will or no, will do what is in the interests of their common welfare; that is, either voluntarily or constrained by force or necessity, they will all live as reason prescribes.   (*Political* 6.3)

STRIVING FOR POWER

Occasionally we get a glimpse into the world of the individual concerned only with power. Every thought and action is calculated and assessed by the measure of whether it can be expected to deliver a greater range of control and influence. Sympathy and empathy have no place, except to the extent that they help the power broker to predict the behaviour of saps and suckers. Such glimpses can be terrifying, as we can feel our moral boundaries lifting and our expectations of fairness peeling away. But the sense of moral vertigo is at the same time thrilling. We may feel, with Nietzsche, that we have stepped beyond both good and evil, and we see what it would be to concern ourselves only with the universe's single genuine currency: *making things happen*. Anything is possible, and all is permitted.

When we feel this vertigo, are we catching a glimpse of some inhuman possibility residing in us? Or are we seeing through the sham of morality to a very real and, indeed, very human possibility? Are we finally seeing through the illusory mist of morality in which we have been nourished? Or are we seeing only a dark temptation, a route we cannot follow, while being at the same time genuine human beings?

Spinoza, as we have seen, understands each individual as a quantum of power interested solely in its own preservation and strength. The striving for power is what unites components into an individual. The extent to which an individual succeeds is its virtue and its freedom, and the individual's failures are instances of bondage and slavery. The "free man", according to Spinoza, is the one who undergoes no changes except what his *conatus* demands. The free man's life, then, is the acquisition of power after power, never fading, and never ceasing. Spinoza affirms that the human essence – as with the essence of all natural individuals – is the pursuit of power, and he does not blink.

In this chapter I shall first describe the morality of the free human, Spinoza's ideal agent, and then explain the ways in which that ideal must be adjusted as it becomes submerged in a real political community. I shall then turn towards Spinoza's advice for constructing the best (i.e. most free and stable) political state, followed by an evaluation of its merits. Finally, we shall see that, when even our best efforts fail, the mind of Spinoza's sage can always retreat into an eternal perspective.

A FREE HUMAN'S MORALITY

Two considerations mark Spinoza's free man apart from the villainous power broker. First, of course, our mind's *greatest* striving is not power and control over others, but seeing and understanding things from an eternal, divine perspective. Gaining power in the world is valuable only to the extent it offers us the leisure and security to gain this conquest and to know and love God. An unruly drive for earthly gain would only distract us from this deeper epistemic striving. And, second, the free man conceived as living in a vacuum and encountering no impediments is pure myth. In this world, as it is and as we are, the smartest strategy we can adopt for preserving ourselves and building up our power is to join a community of like-minded individuals. And this we can do only by agreeing to live sociably, with all attendant social virtues like tolerance, honesty and fair dealing. The scoundrel who is interested only in gain will fare worse overall than will the solid contributor to a greater social good.

Still, the fact remains that we are, at our core, striving for power, and we value others and society only because, in the end, doing so is to our advantage. Spinoza thinks rational self-interest is the mark of reason in an individual. People, as we shall see, are imperfect practitioners of reason, and Spinoza uses this fact to explain the acts of the drunk, the madman and the child. They are each overwhelmed by alien forces that compromise their reason. In so far as we are rational, and act in conformity with our own essence, we act out of self-interest, and acting otherwise is a crime against our nature. Both the social order and morality itself, according to Spinoza, are founded upon the rational self-interest of individuals, and we are in the greatest danger as individuals and as a society when that rationality is overwhelmed by other forces or concerns. As we see in the quote prefacing this chapter, "if human nature were so constituted that men desired most of all what was most to their advantage" – if, in other words, we were all as self-interested as possible – "no special skill would be needed to secure harmony and trust".

In his attempt to illustrate the contours of the right life for human beings, Spinoza demonstrates several features of the free man. Free men think of life, not of death; they have no conception of "good" or "evil", or any sense of "ought" apart from that arising from rationality; they avoid the ignorant; they are grateful to one another; and they always act honestly.[1] In fact, from Spinoza's various remarks about the life of the free man and the life endorsed by rationality, we can assemble a set of maxims of life he would commend to our attention:

1. Do not be surprised when humans act as fools; we are all at the mercy of forces stronger than our own reason.
2. Always strive to understand more.
3. Virtue means doing whatever you can to preserve yourself; *nothing* is more important than that.
4. It is a good idea to form a strong, harmonious community with others. But steer clear of ignorant people.
5. Strive for strength and flexibility in both body and mind.
6. It is always good to be cheerful, and never good to be melancholy.
7. Hate never helps. Repay hate or anger or disdain with love and nobility.
8. Avoid both hope and fear.
9. Do not deceive yourself into thinking anyone is better or worse than they really are, including yourself. So: no pity, flattery, boasting, repentance, or humility.
10. Do not dwell on death. Keep moving forward.

Offering such a quick list – "Spinoza's ten commandments for the free man", as it were – doubtlessly runs the risk of trivializing the thoughts of an extraordinary deep thinker, pulling him down into the ranks of self-help books. But at the same time there can be no doubt that in a work entitled *"Ethics"*, Spinoza was trying to impart moral instruction to his readers; and there should be nothing objectionable about summarizing it and making it handy. The life of rational self-interest Spinoza prescribes is a life consisting in constructive attitudes and honest appraisals, and he argues that it is by living such a life that we are the greatest benefit to one another. "Therefore, men will be most useful to one another, when each one seeks his own advantage, q.e.d." (*Ethics* IVP35C2).

In commenting on his proposition that free men form no conceptions of "good" and "evil", Spinoza assimilates the story of Adam and Eve to his purpose (*Ethics* IVP68S). On his reading, God originally created Adam as a quantum of power seeking his own advantage. But when Adam gained (false or empty) beliefs about good and evil, he began to fear death "rather than desiring to live". Adam then formed a mutually advantageous community with Eve (a smart move!), but soon thereafter began to imitate the affects of the lower, less rational animals, and thereby lost his freedom. The possibility of a return to freedom was "recovered by the Patriarchs, guided by the Spirit of Christ, i.e., by the idea of God, on which alone it depends that man should be free, and desire for other men the good he desires for himself" (*ibid.*). Spinoza's inversion of a more traditional understanding of Genesis 1–3 is remarkable, to say the least: Adam begins with clear knowledge, without any moral illusions; his consumption of the forbidden fruit is his acquisition of the illusory values of "good" and "evil"; God's (or Nature's) "curse" to eat the plants of the field, sweat, turn to dust, and so on, in fact represents Adam's own devolution in rationality, in spite of the rational advantages of his partnership with Eve; and it is the Spirit of Christ (or, *in other words*, the idea of God!) which guides us back to true virtue, that is, the life of rational self-interest. The fact that Spinoza presents this interpretation so deep into *Ethics* IV is, of course, no attempt to make himself sound orthodox in any way. It is rather an attempt to illustrate to the reader that there are ways of retaining some authority of scripture even within Spinoza's radical theology.[2]

Thus does Spinoza place the power broker at Adam's core, and so at the human core. He is ready to deduce what is truly good and what is truly bad from relations of power and consequences of employing power. He is ready to abandon the illusion of there being any transcendent "good" and "evil". But he thinks that, in the end, the society he sketches will embody many familiar virtues, grounded now in a clearer understanding. The task for us now is to see in greater detail how that noble and enlightened society is supposed to arise out of rational self-interest.

STRATEGIC SERVITUDE

A community of Spinozistic sages would establish a harmonious social order with ease. Indeed, it would seem that their only need for government would be to coordinate activity (e.g. to establish a schedule for the use of the commons). But, alas, there is no such ideal community, not since the early days of Adam. Since the time of the Fall from Rationality, when humans began to serve emotions and imagination rather than their own reason, government has been a trickier affair.

We do well to note that Spinoza lived in a time threatening political revolution.[3] For all of his life, the states of the Netherlands were united in a republic, interrupted by frequent invasions and wars. But towards the end of his life, its republicanism was in deep peril. In the 1670s, the Prince of Orange, William III, made a plausible bid to gain monarchical powers over the Netherlands. (He was eventually awarded the highest position of authority [Stadtholder] over the States General, and in 1689 was crowned King William III of England.) Out of concern for this loss of liberty, Spinoza added several chapters on politics to the end of his *Theological-Political Treatise*, and began work on a separate *Political Treatise*. One chief aim of these chapters and this unfinished work was to demonstrate that it is in a republic, and not in a monarchy, that human beings flourish and the greatest possible political stability is achieved. These works also supply Spinoza's answer to the question of how to form a stable and peaceful society of people who are not sages.

It is critical to note first of all that the ceaseless striving for power that is the essence of human individuals never disappears on the political stage, according to Spinoza. We are that striving before we enter the political state, while we are in it and when we leave it. It can no more be traded or bargained away than can a circle's own circularity. Entering into a political state is done precisely because it is to our advantage, and we remain in a state only so far as it contributes towards our advantage (at least, that is, to the extent that we are not subject to irrational forces telling us otherwise). Second, we must note that the power we have at our command is our *right*, as Spinoza understands the term. In other words, we have the *right* to do whatever we *can* do, given our power. Putting these two points together, in a pre-civil condition we have the right to do whatever we can do, and in a civil state we retain that very same right. Indeed, in the civil state we have an even greater right, since we increase the power at our disposal. We cannot possibly give up power as we enter a civil state, because that would be the circle giving up some of its circularity. Our power is only augmented, not traded away, in the transition to the political state.

This foundational feature of Spinoza's political philosophy sets him apart from Hobbes, whose rational agents in a state of nature are willing to relinquish most of their power in a social contract so that there can be a sovereign authority to intimidate us all equally.[4] In Hobbes's civil state, once we have transferred our power to the sovereign, our commitment to obey is equal to the sovereign's ability to enforce. There is, moreover, no possibility of engaging in a rational act of revolution, because the sovereign has such disproportionate power over us that the punishment for revolution would be greater than any discomfort under the sovereign's rule. Thus we avoid the violence and uncertainty of a state of nature in preference to an ordered state in which one authority has far greater power over all of us than any one of us previously commanded. We trade the uncertainty of several bullies for the security of a single greater bully.[5]

In Spinoza's view there is, in the establishment of the civil state, some exchange of powers and rights, but there is no net loss at the level of the individual. The need for a powerful sovereign authority is that, both at home and abroad, not all humans are fully rational. We are pushed and pulled by many forces alien to our own self-interest, which lead us to commit all varieties of violence against one another. "Men can disagree in nature insofar as they are torn by affects which are passions; and to that extent also one and the same man is changeable and inconstant" (*Ethics* IVP33). Knowing this, we see that a sovereign authority that has the power to enforce laws and raise armies is the next-best strategy, given that we cannot be ruled by our own reason. A powerful external authority can get us to do what is *in fact* in our own best interest when passions urge us towards irrational acts. This means, no doubt, that we acquiesce to a relative loss of power, inasmuch as we allow the sovereign to establish a power base, which, in consequence, means we cannot engage in the sorts of behaviours we might have otherwise considered. But we allow (and even applaud) this shift in power only because we see that others will be similarly constrained, and we deem that circumstance to contribute *in a greater way* to our own *conatus* than any other genuine alternative.

In one sense, then, becoming a citizen is *strategic servitude*, or becoming a slave in exchange for greater opportunity to satisfy one's *conatus*. But not in Spinoza's sense of these terms. Freedom, for Spinoza, is not to be understood negatively as simply the absence of obstacles to what one desires. Freedom, as we have seen, is the successful pursuit of one's own striving for self-preservation and power. Even if my superficial desires (for vengeance, for others' possessions, etc.) are frustrated by the sovereign, I am nevertheless free to the extent that my essential striving is satisfied by living in a civil state. Thus, in joining a civil state I augment my freedom, since the state provides me with the security and leisure to follow my own *conatus*. It is not servitude, but liberty from my own irrational desires and the consequences of acting on them.

Although, as we have seen, a perfectly free individual would form no concepts of "good" and "evil", the fact is that Spinoza opens access to these concepts for individuals enmeshed in a world in which things do not always go our way. *Good* for me is that which boosts my power or survival; *evil*, or *bad*, is that which diminishes it. And, as we have also seen, *virtue* in Spinoza's understanding is the successful pursuit of one's self-interest. This affords Spinoza's politics a foundation of naturalized, normative ethics. The state that safeguards its citizens' pursuits of power is making its citizens more virtuous, allowing them to flourish, increasing their freedom and furthering their rights. It is a *good* state, from the perspective of the citizens. Moreover, as we shall see, it is good from the perspective of the state, because it leads to its own greater stability and longevity: that satisfaction of its own *conatus*, so to speak.

Now it may occur to us to object that this view presumes that a sovereign authority will in fact aim at the flourishing of its subjects; and history, let us admit, suffers from a shortage of such sovereign authorities. How may we then be sure that the state does in fact have this aim in mind?

SPINOZA'S REALPOLITIK

It is at this point more important than ever that, in Spinoza's civil state, individuals retain their rights and their power. The citizen's obedience to the state is to be in a state of continuous re-evaluation. Every major legislative decision and law is to be weighed against what powers individuals would command in a state of nature.

This is highlighted by Spinoza's discussion of keeping promises. Writing both about the state of nature and the civil state, Spinoza argues that promises are only as stable as the conditions that make them advantageous to keep:

> If a man has given his pledge to someone, promising only verbally to do this or that which it was within his right [power] to do or not to do, the pledge remains valid for as long as he who made it has not changed his mind. For he who has the power to break faith has in reality not given up his right; he has given no more than words.
>
> (*Political* 2.12)

It is difficult to see any special obligation in keeping promises if they are valid only until the promise-maker changes his mind. The same goes, apparently, for promises or pledges of allegiances to civil states or civil authorities. So long as it is to my advantageous to be a member in good standing in a republic, I will keep my pledge. Of course, in my reckoning I should also factor in the right or power of the state to hunt me down and compel me to keep my pledge. But if I have the power to abandon the state or its laws, and circumstances make it clearly my advantage to do so, then I have the *right* to go my own way; moreover, such disobedience would be *virtuous*, in Spinoza's view. I certainly am not compelled to show up on time for my own hanging, or to turn myself in, or even to volunteer for military service, it seems, if any escape route is available.

Such a stance provides a firm theoretical foundation for rebellion or revolution in a state, precisely when living under the current state is not to our own advantage. This justification of rebellion should constrain a government's legislation. The civil state as an entity and individuals in positions of power retain their power only so far as their rulings are judged by the citizens as advantageous; the citizens are justified in rebelling against policies that exploit or suppress their powers. In other words, the sovereign's own *conatus* will be most successful in its own pursuit of power to the extent that the state works to the advantage of its citizenry. Spinoza puts the point as abstractly and diplomatically as possible:

[T]here are certain conditions that, if operative, entail that subjects will respect and fear the commonwealth, while the absence of these conditions entails the annulment of that fear and respect and together with this, the destruction of the commonwealth. Thus, in order that a commonwealth should be in control of its own right, it must preserve the causes that foster fear and respect; otherwise it ceases to be a commonwealth. (*Political* 4.4)

But shortly after this passage he offers a vivid example: "Then again, to slaughter subjects, to despoil them, to ravish maidens and the like turns fear into indignation, and consequently the civil order into a condition of war" (*ibid.*).

Ideally, then, a smart sovereign would work towards strengthening the rationality and power of its subjects. Their rational obedience is the sovereign's base of power. But here we run into a fixed limitation of human beings, who, as we have seen, typically are more ready to serve emotions and imagination than their own reason. Citizens might well rebel at laws that really do serve their interest, if some passionate orator moves them to do so. So the sovereign must also make use of the next-best available strategy, which is for the state to subjugate passions and imaginations in such a way as to promote the kinds of behaviour that, in fact, contribute to the subjects' own strength and well-being, even if the citizens themselves have no rational understanding of what is in their true interest. The citizens must sometimes be deceived into doing what is in their best interest.

A civic religion is a powerful way of attaining this end. We saw in Chapter 1 that Spinoza provides a set of "dogmas of universal faith", or basic beliefs about God, which we all can agree (one hopes) are taught by scripture throughout its many books. These are beliefs (presented here again for convenience) aimed at motivating a pious lifestyle:

1. There is a God who is supremely just and merciful, or an exemplar of the true life, who should be acknowledged and obeyed as like a judge.
2. God is one and alone, which is a required belief for supreme devotion, admiration and love.

3. God is present everywhere, and is aware of all things.
4. God has power over all things, and is obliged by no one.
5. Worshipping God consists in justice and charity, or in love of one's neighbour.
6. All and only those who worship and obey God are saved.
7. God forgives all those who repent of their sins.

Beyond these basic dogmas, Spinoza urges, people should be allowed to believe and say what they think is true, with utter freedom, and without fear of initiating conflict. But for the sake of the sovereign's power – which, if deployed strategically, also preserves the power of individual citizens – the sovereign should enforce that these dogmas are believed, or at least that citizens act as if they believe them in what they say and do. For "it is not the reason for being obedient that makes a subject, but obedience as such" (*Theological-Political* 17.2).

Generally, the civil state, for its own health and the health of its citizens, must be able to rule over human passions by both punishments and inducements. Spinoza makes the point about punishment in *Ethics* IVP37S2: "In this way Society has the power to prescribe a common rule of life, to make laws, and to maintain them – not by reason, which cannot [by itself] restrain the affects (by P17S), but by threats." A few lines later in the same scholium, Spinoza refashions a religious term to suggest the positive inducements toward obeying the state:

> [T]here is nothing in the state of nature which, by the agreement of all, is good or evil .... So in the state of nature no sin can be conceived.
>
> But in the Civil State, of course, it is decided by common agreement what is good or what is evil. And everyone is bound to submit to the state. *Sin, therefore, is nothing but disobedience*, which for that reason can be punished only by the law of the State. On the other hand, obedience is considered a merit in a Citizen, because on that account he is judged worthy of enjoying the advantages of the State. (*Ethics* IVP17S, emphasis added)

Here and elsewhere Spinoza secularizes the concept of *sin*, so that it is the civil authority, and no religious one, that punishes disobedience. And, correlatively, being without sin means being worthy of the advantages of the state.

What Spinoza proposes, then, is a civic order in which the sovereign's power and the power of the citizenry are reciprocally determined. That arrangement is eminently advantageous and rational to all involved, although it commonly may be that the arrangement needs to be "sweetened" with the images and passions of religion, or noble lies, to get the body politic in harness with the ideals of reason.[6]

MOSES: A CASE STUDY

Near the end of his *Theological-Political Treatise*, Spinoza offers an analysis of the early Hebrew state, based upon his reading of scriptural accounts.[7] He has two reasons for presenting this analysis. The first is once again to show how scripture can be enlisted to support the philosophy he promotes. The second is to illustrate exactly how God (or, more frankly, the natural order of things) favours a state that is established along the lines he has proposed. More particularly, by learning from Moses, we shall learn "what particular concessions sovereign powers must make to their subjects for the greater security and success of their state" (*Theological-Political* 17.3).

The Hebrews, we are told, first organized themselves with God as their absolute monarch. Spinoza claims that once the Hebrews were liberated from Egypt, they transferred their natural right to God. But this initial claim on Spinoza's part makes little sense for two reasons. First, as we have already seen, it is metaphysically impossible for any entity in Spinoza's metaphysics to transfer or relinquish any right, because this would mean denying their own essence, which is a quantum of power. Second, there is no power commanded by any entity that is not already and more properly the power of God. But Spinoza soon makes clear what he really means to say: namely, that while the Hebrews may have held the opinion that they were subordinating themselves to God, they were in fact subordinating themselves to *Moses*. They "absolutely transferred their right to consult God and interpret His edicts to Moses" (*Theological-Political* 17.9). In other words, they agreed individually and among themselves to follow Moses's proclamations, for they had found that in life directly under the rule of God (i.e. *Nature*), they faced many dangers and calamities.

Now, normally, a person in Moses's position would have assumed all the powers of an absolute monarch. And so he did. But Moses wisely foresaw that, as soon as his rule ended, the ensuing power struggle might very well end the nation. So he developed an insightful plan for succession. He first commanded everyone to contribute to a public works project: the construction of the temple. This made all citizens invested in the condition of the temple and (by extension) the welfare of the state. He then selected one of the tribes, the Levites, to have administrative power over the temple, with all its rites and functions, with one of their members (Aaron) serving as the chief priest. He apportioned land to the other tribes, and ordered them to dedicate a portion of their yield to the Levites in order to support them and to show appropriate respect for their governing office. He also raised an army from members of all tribes, seized Canaan, and equitably distributed the new territory among the land-owning tribes. The army was then controlled by a council of leaders from each tribe, with Joshua as their high leader, who communicated with God only through the leader of the Levites. Once Joshua died, the generals from the tribes apparently worked as a council of equals, selecting a higher general only when the territories needed to combine forces against a common foe.

In this way, Moses "chose people to be administrators of the state rather than absolute rulers" (*Theological-Political* 17.14). The supreme Levite priest was not allowed to consult God and issue commands at will, but only when questions and issues were raised by the generals; moreover, the Levites relied on the other tribes for their own power and sustenance. So the power of the priests was checked on two fronts. The generals could consult God as they wished, but only through the supreme priests, so the generals' power was similarly checked. All the people in the various tribes were bound by a single, common religion and by a central civic authority in which they continually invested. In addition, all citizens were obliged to study the laws of the state regularly, which taught them to love the laws, and discouraged administrators from trying to deviate from them. As a result of this network of checks and balances, every unit of society needed to be sensitive towards the other elements and cooperate with them.

Finally, there was a widespread belief that the state was being run just as God would prescribe, and that any enemies of the state were therefore enemies of God. This brought greater courage to the armies as well as greater patriotism among the citizens as a whole. It is certainly no accident that, before Spinoza outlines the history of the Hebrew state, he discusses Alexander's wish to be seen as the son of Jupiter; according to Curtius, Alexander said, "Wars hinge upon reputation; often a false belief has had the same effect as the truth" (*Theological-Political* 17.6). Regarding the Hebrews' calendar of religious holidays and celebrations, Spinoza writes, "Nothing captivates minds more effectively than the cheerfulness arising from devotion, i.e., from love and wonder together" (*Theological-Political* 17.25).

In this way, Spinoza projects the Hebrew state as an ancient precursor to his own United Provinces of Holland: a union of several states, with power distributed throughout the system in such a way as to discourage either rebellion or unilateral oppression by a single element. In effect, Spinoza is arguing that the current state of the Dutch republic is ordained by God, that is, that the nature of human relations in the civil state favours a distributed government with effective checks of power. The threat of reverting to a monarchy should be avoided at all costs.[8]

It remains to be seen why the ancient Hebrew state eventually failed. Spinoza thinks that singling out the Levites as the priestly class, with the understanding that the chief priest was to come from among them, was a fatal mistake. Such favouritism caused envy among the other tribes, and encouraged the Levites to become arrogant in the power they wielded (although it was held in check by other factors). It would have been better to share the temple authority among the tribes equally, perhaps by sending the firstborn from all tribal families to administrate in the temple. This was apparently God's original design (Spinoza refers us to Numbers

8:17). But, the story goes, when all the tribes except the Levites fell to worship the golden calf, the original plan was scrapped, and the authority was bestowed uniquely upon the Levites. Spinoza makes it clear that, in his own reading, elevating the Levites to power is best seen as a *punishment* by God upon the people, rather than as a correction following a terrible mistake. Had the Israelites stayed with the original plan, "all the tribes would have remained far more closely bound to one another, that is, if all had had an equal right to administer the sacred things" (*Theological-Political* 17.27). The moral of the story: do not entrust ecclesiastical authority to a single class of people, but let the administration of sacred things be democratic.

SPINOZA'S REPUBLIC: A LIVE OPTION?

One way to gain a fresh appraisal of Spinoza's republic is to try to envisage what a contemporary republic built from his advice would look like. It would exhibit three global features: (i) the administrative structure would have distinct branches of powers and responsibilities, with the power of each branch checked by the others; (ii) the republic would be broadly tolerant, subject to the state's need for stability; and (iii) the rule of the state would be informed by contemporary science, and especially the social sciences. We shall examine each of these features in turn.

(i) Balanced powers

Spinoza's retelling of the story of Moses is unique in the way he emphasizes Moses's political acumen. Had Moses simply instituted a hereditary line of monarchs, it is likely that the state would have collapsed sooner rather than later: perhaps immediately, in the throes of determining his successor. Instead, Moses appointed administrators and apportioned powers and responsibilities among them so that no single element could unilaterally threaten the stability of the state. He could have done better only had he ensured that members from all tribes were eligible to serve as priests, as that would lower the probabilities of strife among the tribes (and lower the resentment aimed at the Levites).

Hobbes's famous objection against divided government was that it is inevitably unstable; in the end, whoever controls the armed forces rules the land. But Spinoza rightly understands that ruling human societies is more complicated than this. Soldiers are also citizens, with families and children. Moreover, in the case of the Israelites, they experience loyalties to their own tribes as well as to the people as a whole. Whoever tries to command an army to subjugate the soldier's fellow citizens runs the risk of mutiny and civil war. Soldiers and citizens alike desire the peace and protection offered by a stable civil order, and this entails a clear and stable chain of command. If some set of armies among the tribes of Israel decided to revolt against the Levites, they would be violating this chain of command and opening the door to all manner of violent unrest.

There is little that needs to be said today about the advantages of checked powers and divided government. The prescriptive elements of modern political science suggest that the best response to the basic fact that power corrupts is to establish a responsive structure so that the inevitable corruptions can be readily diagnosed and removed. The *offices* are the sovereign, not the holders of those offices. As with Spinoza's physics, the constituent individuals may come and go, and the government will endure, so long as the structure is maintained.

(ii) Toleration, within limits

The citizenry of Spinoza's republic fall into two groups: the sages and the vulgar. No one needs to worry about the sages, Spinoza thinks. Their reason tells them how to behave and when to obey, and as they can be counted upon to serve their own *conatus*, their good citizenship is, for the most part, assured. But then there are the vulgar, ruled predominantly by their passions and fancies. Boundaries must be established to keep the vulgar from destroying the civic order. This, as we have seen, is done with both carrot and stick. Religion, combined with patriotic themes and images, will induce the vulgar to love the state and its laws, and the fear of detection and retribution will induce them to obey the laws. So long as the citizens commit to a minimal set of religious beliefs (the universal dogmas), and also behave in conformity with those beliefs and with the laws of the state, the citizens can think and say as they please.

We may have two very different responses to Spinoza's proposal. First, we will happily applaud his liberal attitude towards thought and speech, especially given his time and place. As he says with Tacitus, times are happy when people can think as they please and say what they think (*Theological-Political*, preface 14). One of his main arguments for this liberal conclusion is consequentialist: he believes that any government that attempts to restrict the thought and speech of its citizenry will necessarily be violent and oppressive, and thereby cause more unrest than if the government simply allowed free expression:

> How much better it would be to restrain the indignation and fury of the common people than issue decrees which cannot but be broken by those who love virtue and the arts, and render the state so narrow-minded that it cannot subsequently tolerate men with free minds! What *greater ill* can be devised for any commonwealth than for honest men to be banished like outlaws because they think differently from the rest and do not know how to hide this? What is *more dangerous*, I contend, than for people to be treated as enemies and led off to death, not for misdeeds or wrongdoing, but because they make a free use of their intelligence, and for the scaffold which should be the terror only of wrongdoers to become a magnificent stage on which to exhibit to all a supreme exemplum of constancy and virtue while casting the deepest reproach on the sovereign?
>
> (*Theological-Political* 20.13, emphasis added)

Sticks and stones must be policed, but words should travel freely in Spinoza's republic.[9]

But, next, we will certainly object to the manipulative and deceitful attitude of his republic to the "vulgar" citizens. His republic is willing to *deceive* and *compel* its citizenry into obedience, by any effective means. But consider this: is anyone willing to deny Spinoza's premise, namely, that in any civil state, we are likely to find a large population of citizens who are more likely to be swayed by irrational passions than by informed and rational judgement? It certainly would be nice if this were not so, and we should work tirelessly toward improving the situation, but there is reason to believe that this fact will not ever change. What then *ought* a republic do in order to ensure its own peaceful stability? Is it better to simply pretend that the unpredictable passions of the vulgar are not a problem?

It might be. Perhaps an overt attempt by any modern government to feed its citizens slogans, films, songs and literature aimed at making them love the state's laws will do more to incite hot rebellion than simply letting the vulgar go their own erratic ways, throwing them into jail whenever they are judged as having broken any actual laws. It may be that any modern state's success at policing its citizens in this way is far more effective and efficient than anything known to Spinoza, and this may explain why he believed a stable community would need additional "internalized agents" (i.e. indoctrination) to shape and police civic behaviour. The same goes for Plato, and his perceived need for the Noble Lie: a society with effective law enforcement has no need for "the invisible watchdog" leashed up to citizens' minds through superstition and myth.

But let us consider this further. What if there were a way to *subtly* encourage citizens toward truly virtuous civic behaviour by engaging their passions and imaginations? Think here not of billboards proclaiming "Big Brother Loves You!", but something like libraries putting up posters with celebrities urging children to read. A state might provide incentives for media organizations to create works that imaginatively (and perhaps covertly) dispose citizens to value justice, civic freedom, toleration, respect for others and the balanced structure of a democratic republic. Producers of media today (to say nothing of campaign specialists) know the science of creating images and tunes that stay in viewers' minds and plant the desire for more of the same. Would it obviously be wrong to harness this science in the direction of better citizenship? The aim would be not to brainwash but to inspire a civic orientation in an individual that would be more likely to develop over time into a more educated and informed outlook.

One might say this "softer" approach is in fact not a noble lie, but *civic education*. The difference between the two is that a noble lie focuses only on securing obedience, while with civic education the aim is to cultivate autonomous thought and capability. Younger students need to be prepared for what they will learn later, and sometimes this preparation means cultivating the right attitudes and values through imaginative and emotional appeals. We share with them inspiring but simplified and less-than-truthful stories of overcoming adversity, fighting evil forces, heroic action, and so on. Our overarching goal in this case is not merely obedience, but, finally, reasoned and autonomous endorsement of the values we have tried to instil in them with myths and stories. In this way, education aims ultimately at strengthening the individual, not brainwashing or enslaving them. But this is precisely Spinoza's goal as well. The measures he advocates encourage citizens to be active, contributing members of civil society, since it is slavery to be in the sway of the passions that fuel uncivil action. He wants us all to "live the life reason prescribes", whether or not we understand how reason prescribes it. Spinoza is perhaps more ready than the rest of us to admit that, in many cases, the final goal of education – rational autonomy – simply will not be reached. Some citizens will remain stubbornly in a condition where they are swayed only by passion and images. His advice to a republic is to continue to shape their behaviour with the same sort of appeals so as to promote their civic obedience, which in fact is in their best interests and promotes their own freedom, whether they recognize this or not.

Democracies throughout history offer countless examples of citizens being manipulated in one way or another, although in recent times the science and technology of manipulation have grown to unprecedented strength. Spinoza's proposed republic would suggest to us that, as a society, it would be better for us not to ignore or suppress this manipulation, but to gain some limited control over this manipulation for the sake of preserving the citizens' freedom and strength. The proposal is not obviously a bad idea.

(iii) Naturalized politics

Spinoza's republic is built upon his own understanding of human social psychology. Modern social psychology is continuous with Spinoza's efforts, tracing causes and building natural explanations for people's behaviour. Although obviously there is much to discover, we have at our disposal an advanced science of human behaviour, and the question is whether or how it should be employed in politics.

For example, consider the fact that most modern democratic states exist in a tension between liberals and conservatives. At least one social psychologist has suggested that the difference between these groups emerges from the varying emphases they place on a fixed set of values, such as caring for others, fairness, individual liberty, group loyalty, respect for authority and respect for sacred things (see Haidt 2012). Everyone shares these values to some degree, but liberals tend to place greater weight on the first three, especially caring for others; and conservatives, while they also value caring for others, place greater emphasis than do liberals on the last three values (loyalty, authority and sanctity). These differences in emphasis tend to get exaggerated in the public space into more dramatic and passionate differences, which lead to familiar, rancorous debates. But taking such facts of human psychology into account could well prompt a modern political state to begin to enquire into the sources of these differences, and to explore what compromises might be engineered that would respect these differences. Moreover, such an enlightened state would try to emphasize the overlap in values among its citizens and strive to reduce fruitless conflict. But this enlightened state would become possible only if there were a radical shift in political perspective: the shift would be away from the "us vs. them" view on the ground to a more detached view of the dynamics of social psychology. The shift would be from political strategy to psychology of politics, under a shared aim of the stability and longevity of the state.

Similarly, as we come to understand the psychology of judges and juries, the enlightened state would come to re-evaluate current judicial practices.[10] We know better than ever how to "stack" juries and sway jurors, and these efforts seldom have anything to do with rational persuasion or reasoned reflection over evidence. But why should our judicial system be blind to the various forces of social psychology at play in its courts? The ideals of justice, including impartial judges and deliberative jurors, are utterly hollow if the judicial process does not in some way use current science to compensate for human passions and our propensity to believe fallacies.

The policies of Spinoza's republic would thus be shaped by knowledge of social psychology. At worst, this raises the same concerns of manipulation and deceit seen in the previous section. In the end, Spinoza's chief answer to those worries is his foundational claim that the rationality of a political state and its actors will dictate that the state do everything in its power to ensure stability and longevity, and that this end is best achieved by following Moses's advice to establish administration rather than appoint rulers. Spinoza's republic would orient itself with respect to "external indicators" of its own health, for example, economic development, health and longevity of its citizens, and their happiness, and so on. Whatever science could help to bring about those ends would be employed.

Spinoza would be the first to admit that this is an ideal, and real states always fall short. But his promise is that, to the extent states approximate Spinoza's republic, they will survive and flourish, just as individuals will flourish to the extent that they follow his ethics. Our brief review in this section indicates that his proposal is indeed a live option.

WHEN ALL ELSE FAILS

Being a student of history, Spinoza knew he could not expect humans to behave rationally or states to compel them to do so. In the end, the sage's chief priority is to safeguard his own liberty, which means his ability to direct his mind freely without interference from others. And sometimes all the sage can do is insulate his life from the uncertainties of political unrest.

It is for this reason that so many of Spinoza's readers have taken him to endorse a life of independent and solitary reflection, despite the fact that Spinoza himself had many friends and engaged so deeply in political philosophy. Everything finally comes down to the individual directing her mind to the one substance and its necessitation of all things. Once we gain the opportunity for sustained reasoning and reflection, this is a good that stands independently of others. We value friends and lovers only to the extent that their support gives us this opportunity, so in the end the individual's pursuit of the very highest good is a solitary one. This must have been born of Spinoza's own experience, as he was turned out from his first community and never fully at home in his second one. He crafted his radical theology largely in one kind of isolation or another. All indications suggest he found solace in this and lived equitably with others, although often distant from them in spirit.

In this way his life and his philosophy serve as iconic representations of the politics of the philosopher. The philosopher is always ready to sketch the contours of the rational state, or at least the one best suited to human nature as it is. When that state is not locally available (and it never is), then the philosopher retreats to a world where reason rules: the world of the mind, or the world created by a book of philosophy. It is the only way to safeguard the sovereignty of reason. When that retreat is not possible, owing to real-world chaos or an individual's own despair, the philosopher disappears and is replaced by either a real-world scrapper or a poet. Philosophy requires, for its own existence, a space in which reason rules. As Bertrand Russell wrote:

> Spinoza's principle of thinking about the whole, or at any rate about larger matters than your own grief, is a useful one. There are even times when it is comforting to reflect that a human life, with all that it contains of evil and suffering, is an infinitesimal part of the life of the universe. Such reflections may not suffice to constitute a religion, but in a painful world they are a help towards sanity and an antidote to the paralysis of utter despair.
>
> (Russell [1945] 1972: 580)

Conclusion

Spinoza vs Nietzsche

"Where is God?" he cried; "I'll tell you! *We have killed him*
– you and I! We are all his murderers. But how did we do
this? How were we able to drink up the sea? Who gave us
the sponge to wipe away the entire horizon? What were
we doing when we unchained this earth from its sun?"

(Nietzsche [1882] 2001: §125)

NATURALISMS

Spinoza may have been the first philosopher to propose a metaphysical vision that so thoroughly integrates the deep reverence
in ancient religion with the remorseless necessity of modern physics. He saw that nature is closed – no loopholes, no exceptions
and no magic – and indifferent to our plight. But he also experienced something divine in nature that had been discerned as well
in revealed religion, although not in full clarity. He proposed not
a compromise, but an integration: yes, nature is as cold and indifferent as a mechanistic physics implies, and, yes, the light of scripture is an expression of the reverence due to nature. He asked that
metaphysics and religion take a step forwards and together into a
synthesis that preserved the essence of each.

Nietzsche, of course, provided a quite different response to the apparent collision between ancient religion and the workings of the natural world, and he commanded a step forwards in a very different direction. Our knowledge of nature, human nature, and human history should alert us to the fact that all forms of religious reverence are due to one pathology or another. We must step past the divine, and indeed past anything that is born of an attempt to provide our lives here and now with an alibi. *Become who you are*, that is, who you are when shorn of ideologies, superstitions, wishful thinking and delusional thinking. The only attitude amounting to reverence is the triumphant thrill we feel in embracing our own lives' conditions, willing them from eternity and to eternity.

"Spinoza vs Nietzsche" is a dramatic and extreme dichotomy, but it is no more than what we face as we pursue the deepest consequences of the most widely shared metaphysics of our age, which is philosophical naturalism. Naturalism is the view that the world is as it appears to the ongoing natural and social sciences, and that there is nothing in reality that is in principle unknowable by these sciences. That is not to say, of course, that our sciences today have everything right; science works by hypotheses and experiments, and we should expect theories to be overturned and explanations to be revised. But all these changes come from within the natural and social sciences themselves, so none of them challenge the underlying presumption that science provides our epistemological access to the nature of reality. There is and can be no *a priori* argument for philosophical naturalism, as providing it would undermine its conclusion. But there could not be greater empirical evidence for naturalism, as our understanding of everything we can experience in nature accelerates with each passing day.

The question we face is how (or whether) to relate naturalism to the divine. Either we follow Spinoza and recognize something divine at the heart of nature, or we follow Nietzsche and step beyond the divine. Philosophical naturalists either find God or they kill God; there really is no middle ground. Of course, anyone might find nature marvellous and at times awe-inspiring, but such an attitude does not amount to the recognition of anything as truly divine; at most, it means we find nature very, very pretty. If our rapture over nature's wonders grows to such a point that we begin to quote Whitman –

> Why should I wish to see God better than this day?
> I see something of God each hour of the twenty-four, and each moment then,
> In the faces of men and women I see God, and in my own face in the glass ...
> ("Song of Myself", §48; Whitman [1855–91] 2004: 64)

– then, yes, perhaps we have discerned something divine in nature. But it is at that point that we should turn back to Spinoza to find some expression of what exactly it is we are venerating. So our choice is stark: do we join Spinoza in unifying nature with God or do we join Nietzsche in ridding nature of God?

At the very least, it is worthwhile to explore the possibility of preserving a space for the divine within the world as understood through naturalism. In this conclusion I shall first argue that, if one wants both naturalism and some positive role for the divine, then one must follow Spinoza, at least in the spirit if not in the letter of his metaphysics. I shall then explore our own naturalism, and argue that any variant of it that does not include the divine must be Nietzschean (again, in spirit at least, if not in letter). I shall then advertise some of the attractions of Spinoza's position. Finally, I shall then conclude with a very brief recommendation to preserve "the infinite", in the sense of "the wondrous", in our philosophy. The chief aim of this conclusion is to encourage philosophers, in a general way, to see through to the depths of our commitments, and to own up to what we are either affirming or abandoning. The stakes, I shall claim, are very high indeed.

MISSING ALTERNATIVES?

Is there really no way to integrate a sense of the divine with naturalism other than to follow Spinoza? What of all the religions in the world that seem to propose other kinds of compromise?

Admittedly, there is always room for a religion that venerates some supernatural divine person who has no causal impact whatsoever upon the world. Naturalism, by its very nature, cannot rule out the possibility of some divine agency that does nothing to affect anything we measure or experience. But anyone who regards such an epiphenomenal deity as worthy of reverence must be exceedingly rare.

Any other form of spirituality or religion will suggest that divine forces or entities *do* affect our world and our experience in ways we can discern. But the trick, then, is to allow this without denying naturalism. So long as one affirms naturalism, one affirms the claim that there are no phenomena that (in principle) are beyond the reach of the sciences. This means all phenomena can be explained as natural phenomena. What room is there, then, for any divine agency to be the cause of any phenomena of our world? Would the divine agency contribute some causal force that somehow runs parallel to the natural causes, but which need not be appealed to in order to understand the phenomena? If so, then this seems little different, in the end, from the epiphenomenal deity just described; although in this case, the deity is contributing something after all, something we need take no notice of.

Or is the divine agency contributing *something* to the phenomena that cannot be explained naturally? In this case, of course, naturalism is shown to be false. Some event or aspect or property in the natural world cannot be explained, even in principle, by science. In short: there is magic. It would be a fool's errand to try to show that in no corner of the universe is there ever any magic (although Spinoza, as we saw in Chapter 1, thought he could pull it off, by appeal to God's constant nature); but at the same time, believers must weigh in their hearts the possibility of genuine magic against the possibility of nature being trickier than we typically imagine (just as Hume suggested). In any case, there is here no alternative that reconciles naturalism with a sense of the divine.

It does not help to sequester the magic to the feelings in one's own heart, as someone might when they believe, "There may be no external evidence for God's existence, but the feelings of my heart tell me of the divine." For emotions are events no less real and natural than photosynthesis. Either there is a natural, psychological explanation for them or not. If there is, then they provide little evidence for divine agency. If there is not, then we are back to magic.

What is left is the Spinozistic alternative: nature is nature, and what it does is itself something divine. Obviously, someone seizing this alternative may depart from Spinoza's own metaphysics in some or many particulars, but in the end the deep and meaningful connection to Spinoza's metaphysics cannot be dodged.

OUR OWN NIETZSCHEAN NATURALISM

In the late 1870s, as Nietzsche emerged from the fog of Wagner's romanticism, he sobered himself with a plunge into the natural causes of human attitudes, beliefs and emotions. He did his best to be utterly ruthless in tearing out any yearning for the transcendent from the human heart and diagnose it as an inevitable and "all-too-human" consequence of thoroughly natural factors:

> That which we now call the world is the outcome of a host of errors and fantasies which have gradually arisen and grown entwined with one another in the course of the overall evolution of the organic being, and are now inherited by us as the accumulated treasure of the entire past.
> (Nietzsche [1878–80] 1996: §16)

He does indeed mean "treasure", because all of these errors and fantasies either sustained and preserved us or provided us with some opportunity for growth in our powers and sensibilities. But he does mean "errors", too. We have got nature and ourselves profoundly wrong. Our only corrective is a sceptical, scientific attitude, searching for dispassionate causes and blind mechanisms. We must even carry this attitude as we explore the grounds of science itself, because scientists are also all too human and are sometimes victims of their own human delusions. His advice to us is to seek out *especially* that which we revere, and understand how we have deceived ourselves into revering it. We shall know we have succeeded when no idol is left standing.

135

The only value Nietzsche retains is a striving he finds in life itself: the will to power, or a striving in living organisms to augment their own strength. As living organisms, we are stuck with this striving. Any ascetic urge to overcome it in ourselves is born of some pathology, such as a perverse attempt to impress others with our strength by denying ourselves what everyone else commonly desires. But although Zarathustra sings songs about life, and Nietzsche writes rapturously about it, he understands it to be at bottom a cold, objective fact about what animates us as organic beings, and a force powerful enough to distort everything we see and value. "When we speak of values, we speak under the inspiration, under the optics of life: life itself is forcing us to posit values, life itself is valuing by means of us, *when* we posit values" (Nietzsche [1889] 1997: §5.5).

Although no one writes like Nietzsche anymore, our contemporary naturalists share his fervour to bring down idols. Natural selection has given us our hardware, and any hard-wired values that no amount of talking will take away. Each of these features (like love for offspring, and distaste for rotten meat) are with us now because at some time in the past they conferred upon our ancestors some advantage in producing offspring who lived long enough to reproduce again. This, of course, gives us no *reason* to value them; it only provides a *causal* explanation of why we ended up valuing them. On top of the hard-wired values, there are long-standing cultural practices and ideologies that have successfully reproduced themselves, generation after generation, through us (like keeping promises, or shunning cheaters): we have carried them along with us and passed them along like viruses or parasites. Again, this history of success gives us no *reason* to value them; it only explains how we have come to value them. And on top of the long-standing cultural values, there are relatively more recent ideas and fads that are now having a go at becoming longtimers, and we shall see what their reproductive longevity turns out to be (like owning property, and denouncing racism). We live in the intersection of many kinds of value structures, in our hardware and software, and the only "value" they have, on a naturalist account, rests in their success at reproducing themselves through us. We have no *reason* to value anything, although we certainly have *cause* to.

If I seem heavy-handed about this, it is only because very often our naturalists do not seem to recognize the utterly arbitrary nature of human values, according to their own account. Their attitude seems to be that if a natural account can be given of a particular human value, then that value has been shown to be both real and natural; and if this is achieved, then we have found reason to sustain it and act on its behalf.[1] But this attitude can be tested against thought experiments involving our newly acquired abilities to change human hardware and software. Suppose, for example, we find ways to genetically engineer humans not to feel love towards their offspring; suppose we find ways to engineer societies in which some default level of trust is not required, and children are not taught to have it; suppose we engineer a society with a race of slaves who are bred and taught to take delight in their servitude. In these dystopic societies, the new values would be every bit as "natural" as the values we now possess. True, they did not evolve over millennia on the savannahs; but surely savannah values are not the only "natural" values for humans to have. Shall we say, then, that those new values are equally legitimate, and that the only reason we feel revulsion at them is because of the arbitrary set of values we happen to have inherited? What gives savannah values any special authority, other than the fact that we find ourselves with them now?

The true naturalist is ready for all of this objection, and is ready to disown any absolute foundation that makes one set of values more legitimate than another. Nietzsche was such a naturalist, and he ended up scaring even himself:

> One day there will be associated with my name the recollection of something frightful – of a crisis like no other before on earth, of the profoundest collision of conscience, of a decision evoked *against* everything that until then had been believed in, demanded, sanctified. ...
>
> He who unmasks morality has therewith unmasked the valueness of all values which are or have been believed in; he no longer sees in the most revered, even *canonized* types of man anything venerable, he sees in them the most fateful kind of abortion, fateful *because they exercise fascination.* (Nietzsche [1889] 1992: §15.1, §15.8)

But in popular discussions of naturalizing values today, we rarely see any expression or recognition of such a profound collision of conscience. Perhaps the timescales required for monumental changes in our values are too large to occasion any sharp and immediate concern. Or perhaps naturalists are placing upon our values' natural origins (i.e. the savannahs) some special kind of moral privilege, or some sense that because the values we have inherited have been inherited through a long period of evolution, that indeed makes them truly valuable. Or perhaps, most likely of all, no one is thinking as deeply as Nietzsche thought.

SPINOZA'S DIVINE NATURALISM

Nietzsche found in Spinoza a kindred spirit. In a letter to his friend Overbeck in 1881, Nietzsche wrote:

> I am really amazed, really delighted! I have a precursor, and what a precursor! I hardly knew Spinoza .... [T]his most abnormal and lonely thinker is close to me in these points precisely: he denies free will, purposes, the moral world order, the nonegotistical, evil .... *In summa*: my solitariness which, as on very high mountains, has often, often made me gasp for breath and lose blood, is now at least a solitude for two.   (Nietzsche [1861–89] 1996: 177)[2]

Nietzsche got Spinoza right: he did deny all those things. Like Nietzsche, Spinoza also tried to dispassionately diagnose all of the illusions and snares we set for ourselves. And, in an especially striking parallel, Spinoza also set a certain striving at the essence of all natural beings, although it was not a will to power, but a striving to persevere.

But unlike Nietzsche, Spinoza found something divine at the heart of nature. The first part of his *Ethics* is dedicated to the existence and nature of the one substance; the last part is dedicated to the life in greatest harmony with the one substance. Clearly, the divine substance is not a person, has no providence or plans, does not judge people or actions as good or evil, and will not hear any prayers or songs. And yet Spinoza calls it "God" and, wherever he can, he connects his concept to scripture. Prayer and worship is not appropriate for Spinoza's God, but *intellectual love* is. When Spinoza demonstrates that the mind's intellectual love of God is the same love with which God loves himself (*Ethics* VP36), Spinoza is not playing with words. He is describing an intellectual union with a divine being more profound and enriching than Moses's experience, whatever it was, on the mountain.

Naturalists may speak today of the beauty and wonder of nature but few, if any, regard nature as divine. This may be in part because, in many minds, "divine" may connote various spiritual miracles or special benefits coming our way, and naturalism at its core denies that humans have any privileged relation to nature. Of course, Spinoza denies this sense of the divine, and believes nature is both divine and uncaring with regard to human fate. Naturalists may also worry what they would be committing themselves to in calling nature divine: would this commit them to denying the second law of thermodynamics, or to life after death, or to reincarnation? But Spinoza's naturalism does not decree that we will find in nature anything other than the sorts of laws and mechanisms science already posits. It is just that the final object we are coming to understand as we understand nature is itself divine.

But one might well wonder what this does for us. What gain is there for us in seeing nature as divine? Although Spinoza never argued for his view in this way (in an analysis of benefits), it is clear that one "gain" is that we see our own existence as enfolded in a final, complete structure that could not possibly be otherwise. Our existence does not follow from the decree of some divine person, but neither is it as arbitrary and valueless as Nietzsche would have it. We *belong* here. We are, in our essence, identical with a single power for existence from which everything arises, and to which everything returns. In so far as we grasp this, we unite our minds with a cosmic joy, which is the joy of sheer power-to-be. Nietzsche's positive prescription – to embrace and say "Yes!" to the conditions of one's own existence – is a yes-saying that follows a great no-saying: no to transcendence, no to God, and no to absolute value. Spinoza's living philosophy is quite different. The more we understand, the more illusions we discard, and the more love we feel towards what we find. It is not a play in two parts (no and yes), but a continuous journey into ultimate reality. In Nietzsche's universe we must fashion our own home, while in Spinoza's we discover ourselves to be already at home.

It may seem to some that this talk of feeling love and finding home in the universe sounds silly, naive and childish. That may just mean we are more with Nietzsche than with Spinoza. We do not see the universe, and our existence in it, as ultimately anything other than sound and fury, signifying nothing. That is just to say that we do not find nature to be divine in Spinoza's sense, and – particularly after the horrors of the twentieth century – it may well be that is the only "choice" left us. As the next section will show, I hope that is not so.

PRESERVING THE INFINITE

Philosophy begins in wonder, according to Socrates in Plato's *Theaetetus*. But our word "wonder" isn't strong enough. Socrates knew wonder as Thaumas, a god of the ocean. So we should have in mind the wonder we experience when we are brought to consider the ocean's great size to our own small compass. When Socrates spoke of Thaumas, he said it was a gifted genealogist who claimed that Thaumas's daughter was Iris, the messenger of the gods. Perhaps he meant that when we are brought to that kind of wonder – standing at the end of the boundless – perhaps we are then in a position to feel intimations of the divine. Perhaps this wonder at existence itself is the message from the gods.

Now Spinoza had little regard for wonder (Latin "*admiratio*"), at least in one sense of the term. He used the term "*admiratio*" to refer to the slack-jawed astonishment with which we behold a single thing we cannot understand ("imagination of a singular thing, insofar as it is alone in the Mind"; *Ethics* IIP52S). Wonder in this sense is a non-productive, ignorant state that does little more than stop us in our tracks. It is far better to adopt an approach of curiosity in the hope of coming to understand the wondrous thing. But there is another kind of positive affective wonder that Spinoza placed great value upon. As we have seen, Spinoza believed our greatest satisfaction of mind is in the intellectual love of God, identifying it as "our salvation, or blessedness", which the scriptures called "glory" (*Ethics* VP36S). In this state, we come to understand our knowledge to be the very love with which the one substance loves itself. It is an immediate awareness of our deep union with the infinite intellect. *We are it.* This is a species of wonder rooted in knowledge, not in ignorance.

It seems to me that, in our philosophizing, we must always be wary of reducing or explaining away the very elements of our experience that compel us to philosophize in the first place. Philosophies derive their value from their success in capturing the significance of what we know to be most important before we ever begin to philosophize. Philosophies that get fundamental values wrong, or have no space for them, thereby mark themselves out as failures. Doubtlessly, philosophy will show *some* of the ideals we once cherished to be hollow illusions, or even contradictions. That is what it is to value truth. But there are limits to what in our experience we can disown. T. S. Eliot, thinking primarily of moral attributes, called this fact to our attention:

> [I]f certain emotional states, certain developments of character, and what in the highest sense can be called "saintliness" are inherently and by introspection known to be good, then the satisfactory explanation of the world must be an explanation which will admit the "reality" of these values. (Quoted in Trilling 2000: 26)[3]

The same is true, I should think, of certain philosophical states, especially the ones that seem to us to connect us to larger wholes that bring meaning into our lives. The exalted experiences that Plato calls "wonder", and Spinoza calls "*amor intellectus dei*", are just of this sort. We should act to preserve them in our philosophies, because without them human experience itself becomes something unremarkable and unworthy of philosophical examination. Since I do not know how to argue for this claim, I can only try to evoke that sense of wonder itself, and ask whether anyone could possibly want to deny its authenticity.

We do well to recognize the nobility of any ideals we renounce. And, as Spinoza well knew, we do even better to hold off a bit before finally renouncing them.

141

Notes

PREFACE

1. "God-intoxication", of course, refers to Novalis's calling Spinoza a "God-intoxicated man".
2. I am thinking here principally of Donagan (1988), James (2012) and Mason (1997), although there are surely others, and many others who agree partway.

INTRODUCTION

1. I am using "myth" in its most common sense, as an account that is largely imaginative and does not work very well when it is used in the ways we try to use scientific theories (e.g. for prediction, theoretical unification, and so on). Myths may be useful in other important ways, of course: they can help orient lives, provide values, give purpose, and so on. But they make for poor science.
2. For an excellent overview of these issues, see Kugel (2007).
3. From Voltaire's "Epistle to the Author of the Book, *The Three Imposters*". It is surprisingly difficult to find English translations of this work in print; here is the context of the famous quote, as found in Voltaire ([1768] 2012, emphasis added):

   If the heavens, stripped of his noble imprint,
   Could ever cease to attest to his being,
   If God did not exist, it would be necessary to invent him.
   Let the wise man announce him and kings fear him.
   Kings, if you oppress me, if your eminencies disdain

The tears of the innocent that you cause to flow,
My avenger is in the heavens: learn to tremble.
Such, at least, is the fruit of a useful creed.

4. Indeed, the more timid readers of Nietzsche work desperately to show that, somehow, our old moral notions will remain in place even after we have rejected the superstitions justifying them to us. But just as some biblical interpreters have tried to read modern morals into an ancient text, these scholars are trying to read ancient morals into a modern text.

5. See Nadler (2011) and Israel (2001) for excellent accounts of Spinoza's treatise, its reception and its legacy. Curley (1990) and Melamed (2010) also demonstrate how much of Spinoza's metaphysics can be seen in the treatise, or inferred directly from it.

1. READING SCRIPTURE RIGHTLY

1. Interestingly, Meijer's work was initially thought to be a work by Spinoza; see Laerke (2010: 116–17).

2. On the basis of Deuteronomy 5:4, "The Lord spoke with you face to face at the mountain in the midst of the fire", although (weirdly) this is Moses speaking to the Israelites, none of whom were on the mountain with Moses. Moses does go on to say "I stood between the Lord and you at the time". The Lord seems especially keen to communicate directly only with Moses, so it is puzzling why Spinoza should be so confident that Moses's experience is veridical.

3. Indeed, Exodus 33:11 reads: "Thus the Lord used to speak to Moses face to face, as a man speaks to his friend"; but the Lord later tells Moses that "you cannot see my face; for man shall not see me and live" (Exod. 33:20).

4. "By this we know that we abide in him and he in us, because he has given us of his own Spirit" (1 John 4:13). Spinoza chose this passage as the prefatory quote for the *Theological-Political Treatise*.

2. GOD, AS KNOWN BY REASON

1. This objection was first raised by Della Rocca (2002), although he provides a different answer to it.

2. This same thought is repeated in the *Short Treatise*, part I, ch. 1, note b (Curley, 61).

3. See Wolterstorff (1991). Furth (1988) also provides a good discussion of inherence. According to Furth, when X inheres in Y, X is not thought of as a property of Y, but X is thought of as an individual that stands in a relation of inherence to Y.

4. "Thence it follows that in God essence is not really distinct from person; and yet that the persons are really distinguished from each other" (Aquinas, *Summa Theologiae* pt 1, q. 39, art. 1). Similarly, in Spinoza's metaphysics, the attributes could be seen as really distinct from one another

(but only in the sense that they are each conceptually self-contained; obviously none can exist without the others, as they are equally essences of a necessary being), although none is really distinct from the essence of God (only conceptually distinct). One perhaps could try to use explications of the Trinity suggested by the scholastics to shed light on Spinoza's doctrine of the many attributes of the one substance; but after studying Aquinas's discussion, I have elected to abandon that worthwhile project to more capable minds.

3. THE GENESIS OF ALL THINGS

1. For a convincing, book-length argument of the importance of the principle of sufficient reason to Spinoza's philosophy, see Della Rocca (2008).
2. At least, as Parmenides is commonly interpreted; for an argument against this interpretation, see Curd (1998).
3. For this reason, Curley thinks Spinoza must be using the term *mode* in a way that breaks sharply with its traditional use. See Curley (1969).
4. The phrase Spinoza employs in his letter to Schuller, "*facies totius universi*", is both unusual and interesting. One wonders whether Spinoza had in mind the Jewish notion of the Shekinah, which can be understood as the face or appearance of God. So, for example, when it is said that God dwells with his people or in the tabernacle (as Exodus 25:8, 29:45), it is the Shekinah that so dwells. Some rabbis have considered the Shekinah as playing a kind of intermediary role between God and the world: it is one way in which God can represent himself to humans. Since Spinoza, in his letter, is answering Schuller's request for an example of a *mediate* infinite mode of God, it may be that the notion of the Shekinah is just the sort of thing he felt he needed to make his point, since both Spinoza's *facies* and the Shekinah are supposed to be, in their own ways, the impersonal manifestation of God in our world.
5. Reluctant, that is, after he learned of Galileo's condemnation. "For", as he wrote Father Mersenne, "I would not for all the world want a discourse to issue from me that contained the least word of which the Church would disapprove" (quoted in Descartes [1619–50] 1985: I, 79).
6. For a more detailed version of this argument, see Huenemann (1999).
7. The idea here is the same as the one employed by Curley (1969: 102–4), although to a different end.
8. In the *Treatise on the Emendation of the Intellect*, §§ 69 and 72 (Curley, 31–2), Spinoza also draws our attention to ideas that are perfectly coherent and legitimate, but that represent objects which "never existed, and never will exist". I do not discuss these passages in the main text because their context is tricky to establish. It seems to me that in this part of the work, Spinoza's concern is more with what makes an idea coherent than with necessitarianism, so he temporarily tolerates claims he elsewhere rejects for other reasons.
9. For a full defence of this view, see Curley & Walski (1999).

10. But it may be that the tension between these two views of Spinoza's necessitarianism can be resolved. For a subtle examination of the issues involved, see Griffin (2008).

11. For more about emanation, see Viljanen (2011: ch. 2), and Des Chene (1996: ch. 5).

12. Later on this same page, Tillich goes on to very briefly *contrast* his view with Spinoza's "naturalistic pantheism", which (to me) is only evidence for thinking Tillich had not studied Spinoza all that deeply, at least on this topic.

4. OUR PLACE IN THE WORLD

1. In fact Spinoza is a little more precise than this with his terms. "Joy" (*laetitia*) and "sadness" (*tristitia*) pertain only to the mind's growth or deficiency in power; "cheerfulness" (*hilaritas*) and "melancholy" (*melancholia*) pertain to body and mind taken together. See *Ethics* IIIP11S. But nothing I shall say will require us to keep this terminology straight.

2. Suicides must then be cases in which external causes – such as the low esteem of others – are the cause of death. For more discussion of *Ethics* IIIP4, and Spinoza's *conatus* doctrine generally, see Garrett (2002).

3. For further discussion of rational knowledge's promise of reaching beyond the imagination, see Huenemann (2008b).

4. Don Rutherford presents a more comprehensive view of Spinoza's general advice here, and puts it into a concise formula: "everything we do, including our efforts to act in accordance with [sound precepts of living], is dictated by [natural necessity]; and we fulfill the requirements of [sound precepts of living], in so far as we understand the world as ordered by [natural necessity]" (Rutherford 2010: 163).

5. The fact that man's greatest good is common to all "arises from the very nature of reason, insofar as that essence is defined by reason, and because man could neither be nor be conceived if he did not have the power to enjoy this greatest good. For it pertains" (*Ethics* IVP36S).

6. For an illuminating and patient account of these themes in *Ethics* V, see Cook (2007: 128–49).

7. My knowledge of Maimon is wholly indebted to Atlas (1959), Beiser (2002) and Melamed (2004).

8. One wonders whether it was for this reason that Tschirnhaus (through Schuller) asked Spinoza whether the attribute of thought ranges more widely than any of the other attributes (*Letters* 70, from Schuller); Spinoza unfortunately never commented on that suggestion.

9. Interestingly, Maimon identified Leibniz's monadic metaphysics as a sort of compromise position occupying a space midway between (on the one hand) Spinoza's and Maimon's acosmism and (on the other) a thoroughly materialistic and deterministic atheism (such as Hobbes's). One may well doubt that Leibniz himself would have enjoyed being characterized in this way as a halfway house between Spinozism and atheism!

5. SPINOZA'S REPUBLIC

1. This claim (*Ethics* IVP72) has puzzled several commentators, as it would seem there are many occasions where deception would do more to enhance one's power than truth-telling. But I believe Spinoza has in mind a community of free men, where all the cards are on the table, and any attempt at deception would fail anyway. For more discussion, see Garrett (1990) as well as Garrett (2010).

2. Spinoza makes similar religious assimilations in the *Ethics* at IIP7S and VP36S.

3. Nadler (1999, 2011) offers excellent broad accounts of Spinoza's political context.

4. "[T]he difference between Hobbes and myself ... consists in this, that I always preserve the natural right in its entirety, and I hold that the sovereign power in a State has right over a subject only in proportion to the excess of power over that of a subject" (*Letters* 50, to Jelles). For further discussion of the relation between Hobbes and Spinoza, see Curley (1996) and Garrett (2010).

5. Locke's criticism of Hobbes's view: "This is to think, that men are so foolish, that they take care to avoid what mischiefs may be done to them by *pole-cats*, or *foxes*; but are content, nay, think it safety, to be devoured by *lions*" (*Second Treatise* 7.93; Locke [1690] 1980: 50).

6. This reciprocal determination is illuminated in James (2012: 247–8). Rosenthal (2010) also explores the possibility of employing images and passions to bring the body politic into order.

7. For a much more comprehensive treatment of these issues, see James (2012: chs 10–12).

8. James (2012: ch. 11) provides ample illustration of the fact that, by Spinoza's day, there was widespread recognition of the United Provinces as the New Zion.

9. As Rosenthal (2001) argues, there is more to Spinoza's endorsement of toleration than merely this consequentialist argument; he sees toleration as a positive virtue of a republic, one that strengthens it, as well as a private virtue in an individual.

10. For further discussion, see Leiter (2007).

CONCLUSION: SPINOZA VS NIETZSCHE

1. There are many examples of this attitude, although a popular one is Harris (2010).

2. Nietzsche soon overcame his initial admiration of Spinoza. Five years later he refers to the *Ethics* as "that hocus pocus of a mathematical form ... how much personal timidity and vulnerability this sick hermit's masquerade reveals!" (Nietzsche [1886] 2002: §6).

3. This is from Eliot's essay *The Idea of a Christian Society* (1939).

Bibliography

Aquinas, T. [1265–74] 1912–25. *The Summa Theologica of St. Thomas Aquinas*, 3 vols, Fathers of the English Dominican Province (trans.). London: Burns, Oates, and Washburne.

Atlas, S. 1959. "Solomon Maimon and Spinoza". *Hebrew Union College Annual* 30: 233–85.

Beiser, F. 2002. *German Idealism: The Struggle Against Subjectivism, 1781–1801*. Cambridge, MA: Harvard University Press.

Cook, J. 2007. *Spinoza's Ethics: A Reader's Guide*. New York: Continuum.

Curd, P. 1998. *The Legacy of Parmenides*. Princeton, NJ: Princeton University Press.

Curley, E. 1969. *Spinoza's Metaphysics*. Cambridge, MA: Harvard University Press.

Curley, E. 1990. "Notes on a Neglected Masterpiece (II): the *Theological-Political Treatise* as a Prolegomenon to the *Ethics*". In *Central Themes in Early Modern Philosophy*, J. Cover & M. Kulstad (eds), 109–59. Indianapolis, IN: Hackett.

Curley, E. 1996. "Kissinger, Spinoza, and Genghis Khan". In *The Cambridge Companion to Spinoza*, D. Garrett (ed.), 315–82. Cambridge: Cambridge University Press.

Curley, E. 2010. "Spinoza's Exchange eith Albert Burgh". See Melamed & Rosenthal (2010), 11–28.

Curley, E. & G. Walski 1999. "Spinoza's Necessitarianism Reconsidered". See Gennaro and Huenemann (1999), 241–62.

Della Rocca, M. 2002. "Spinoza's Substance Monism". See Koistinen & Biro (2002), 11–37.

Della Rocca, M. 2008. *Spinoza*. New York: Routledge.

Descartes, R. [1619–50] 1985. *The Philosophical Writings of Descartes*, 3 vols, J. Cottingham *et al.* (trans.). Cambridge: Cambridge University Press.

Des Chene, D. 1996. *Physiologia*. Ithaca, NY: Cornell University Press.

Donagan, A. 1988. *Spinoza*. Chicago, IL: University of Chicago Press.

Einstein, A. 1954. "Science and Religion". In his *Ideas and Opinions*, 41–9. New York: Crown Publishers.

Fix, A. 1990. *Prophecy and Reason: The Dutch Collegiants in the Early Enlightenment*. Princeton, NJ: Princeton University Press.

Furth, M. 1988. *Substance, Form and Psyche*. Cambridge: Cambridge University Press.

Garrett, D. 1990. "'A Free Man Always Acts Honestly, Not Deceptively': Freedom and the Good in Spinoza's Ethics". In *Spinoza: Issues and Directions*, E. Curley & P.-F. Moreau (eds), 221–38. Leiden: Brill.

Garrett, D. 2002. "Spinoza's *Conatus* Argument". See Koistinen & Biro (2002), 127–58.

Garrett, D. 2010. "'Promising' Ideas: Hobbes and Contract in Spinoza's Political Philosophy". See Melamed & Rosenthal (2010), 192–209.

Gennaro, R. & C. Huenemann (eds) 1999. *New Essays on the Rationalists*. New York: Oxford University Press.

Griffin, M. 2008. "Necessitarianism in Spinoza and Leibniz". See Huenemann (2008a), 71–93.

Haidt, J. 2012. *The Righteous Mind: Why Good People are Divided by Politics and Religion*. New York: Pantheon.

Harris, S. 2010. *The Moral Landscape*. New York: Free Press.

Huenemann, C. 1999. "The Necessity of Finite Modes and Geometrical Containment in Spinoza's Metaphysics". In *New Essays on the Rationalists*, R. Gennaro & C. Huenemann (eds), 224–40. New York: Oxford University Press.

Huenemann, C. (ed.) 2008a. *Interpreting Spinoza*. Cambridge: Cambridge University Press.

Huenemann, C. 2008b. "Epistemic Autonomy in Spinoza". See Huenemann (2008a), 94–110.

Israel, J. 2001. *Radical Enlightenment: Philosophy and the Making of Modernity 1650–1750*. New York: Oxford University Press.

James, S. 2012. *Spinoza on Philosophy, Religion, and Politics*. New York: Oxford University Press.

Koistinen, O. & J. Biro (eds) 2002. *Spinoza: Metaphysical Themes*. New York: Oxford University Press.

Kołakowski, L. 2004. *The Two Eyes of Spinoza*. South Bend, IN: St Augustine's Press.

Kugel, J. 2007. *How to Read the Bible*. New York: Free Press.

Laerke, M. 2010. "G. W. Leibniz's Two Readings of the *Tractatus*". In Melamed & Rosenthal 2010, 101–27.

Leibniz, G. [1675–1716] 1989. *Philosophical Essays*, R. Ariew & D. Garber (trans.). Indianapolis, IN: Hackett.

Leibniz, G. [1666–1716] 1989. *Philosophical Papers and Letters*, L. Loemker (trans.), 2nd edn/second printing. Dordrecht: Kluwer. [Cited as Leibniz/Loemker.]

Leiter, B. 2007. *Naturalizing Jurisprudence*. Oxford: Oxford University Press.

Locke, J. [1690] 1980. *Second Treatise of Government*. Indianapolis, IN: Hackett.

Mason, R. 1997. *The God of Spinoza*. Cambridge: Cambridge University Press.

Meijer, L. [1666] 2005 . *Philosophy as the Interpreter of Holy Scripture*, S. Shirley (trans.). Milwaukee, WI: Marquette University Press.

Melamed, Y. 2004. "Salomon Maimon and the Rise of Spinozism in German Idealism". *Journal of the History of Philosophy* 42: 67–96.

Melamed, Y. 2010. "The Metaphysics of the *Theological-Political Treatise*". See Melamed & Rosenthal (2010), 128–42.

Melamed, Y. & M. Rosenthal (eds) 2010. *Spinoza's* Theological-Political Treatise: *A Critical Guide*. Cambridge: Cambridge University Press.

Menn, S. 1995. "The Greatest Stumbling Block: Descartes' Denial of Real Qualities". In *Descartes and His Contemporaries*, R. Ariew & M. Grene (eds), 182–207. Chicago, IL: University of Chicago Press.

Nadler, S. 1999. *Spinoza: A Life*. Cambridge: Cambridge University Press.

Nadler, S. 2011. *A Book Forged in Hell*. Princeton, NJ: Princeton University Press.

Newport, F. 2007. "One-Third of Americans Believe the Bible is Literally True". www.gallup.com/poll/27682/OneThird-Americans-Believe-Bible-Literally-True.aspx (accessed September 2013).

Nietzsche, F. [1889] 1992. *Ecce Homo*, R. J. Hollingdale (trans.). New York: Penguin.

Nietzsche, F. [1861–89] 1996. *Selected Letters*, C. Middleton (trans.). Indianapolis, IN: Hackett.

Nietzsche, F. [1878–80] 1996. *Human, All Too Human*, R. J. Hollingdale (trans.). Cambridge: Cambridge University Press.

Nietzsche, F. [1889] 1997. *Twilight of the Idols*, R. Polt (trans.). Indianapolis, IN: Hackett.

Nietzsche, F. [1882] 2001. *The Gay Science*, J. Nauckhoff (trans.). Cambridge: Cambridge University Press.

Nietzsche, F. [1886] 2002. *Beyond Good and Evil*, J. Norman (trans.). Cambridge: Cambridge University Press.

Pascal, B. [1669] 1995. *Pensées and Other Writings*, H. Levi (trans.). Oxford: Oxford University Press.

Preus, J. 2009. *Spinoza and the Irrelevance of Biblical Authority*. Cambridge: Cambridge University Press.

Rosenthal, M. 2001. "Tolerance as a Virtue in Spinoza's *Ethics*". *Journal of the History of Philosophy* 39: 535–57.

Rosenthal, M. 2010. "Miracles, Wonder, and the State in Spinoza's *Theological-Political Treatise*". See Melamed & Rosenthal (2010), 231–49.

Russell, B. [1945] 1972. *A History of Western Philosophy*. New York: Simon & Schuster.

Rutherford, D. 2010. "Spinoza's Conception of Law: Metaphysics and Ethics." See Melamed & Rosenthal (2010), 143–67.

Spinoza, B. [1677] 1985. *The Collected Works of Spinoza*, vol. 1, E. Curley (ed. and trans.). Princeton, NJ: Princeton University Press.

Spinoza, B. [1677] 1995. *The Letters*, S. Shirley (trans.). Indianapolis, IN: Hackett.

Spinoza, B. [1677] 2000. *Political Treatise*, S. Shirley (trans.). Indianapolis, IN: Hackett.

Spinoza, B. [1677] 2007. *Theological-Political Treatise*, M. Silverthorne & J. Israel (trans.). Cambridge: Cambridge University Press.

Tillich, P. 1951. *Systematic Theology*, 3 vols. Chicago, IL: University of Chicago Press.

Tillich, P. 1959. "Science and Theology: A Discussion with Einstein". In his *Theology of Culture*, 127–32. New York: Oxford University Press.

Trilling, L. 2000. *The Moral Obligation to be Intelligent*. New York: Farrar, Straus, & Giroux.

Verbeek, T. 2003. *Spinoza's Theological-Political Treatise*. Ashford: Ashgate.

Viljanen, V. 2011. *Spinoza's Geometry of Power*. Cambridge: Cambridge University Press.

Voltaire, F.-M. A. [1768] 2012. "Epistle to the Author of the Book, *The Three Imposters*", http://allpoetry.com/poem/8538281-Epistle__to_the_author_of__The_Three_Impostors_-by-Voltaire (accessed September 2013), J. Iverson (trans.).

Wippel, J. 1982. "Essence and Existence". In *The Cambridge History of Later Medieval Philosophy*, N. Kretzmann, A. Kenny, J. Pinborg & E. Stump (eds), 385–410. Cambridge: Cambridge University Press.

Whitman, W. [1855–91] 2004. *The Portable Walt Whitman*. New York: Penguin.

Wolfson, H. A. [1934] 1962. *The Philosophy of Spinoza*, 2 vols. Cambridge, MA: Harvard University Press.

Wolterstorff, N. 1991. "Divine Simplicity". *Philosophical Perspectives* 5: 531–52.

Index

Printed in the USA/Agawam, MA
August 20, 2014

595407.010